Warming Up and Cooling Down

South Trafford College

Second Edition

Jo Harris, PhD
Loughborough University

Jill Elbourn, MSc
Educational Exercise Consultant

Human Kinetics

Library of Congress Cataloging-in-Publication Data

Harris, Jo, 1955-
    Warming up and cooling down, 2nd edition / by Jo Harris, Jill Elbourn.
        p. cm.
    Includes bibliographical references.
    ISBN 0-7360-3878-7
    1. Physical education for children--Great Britain--Curricula. 2. Exercise--Study and
teaching--Great Britain. I. Elbourn, Jill, 1959- II. Title.

    GV443 .H319 2002
    613.7'071--dc21   2001039844

ISBN: 0-7360-3878-7

Copyright © 2002 by Jo Harris and Jill Elbourn

Acquisitions Editor: Scott Wikgren; **Development Editor:** Diane Evans; **Assistant Editor:** Sandra Merz Bott; **Copyeditor:** Janet Pannocchia; **Proofreader:** Erin Cler; **Graphic Designer:** Nancy Rasmus; **Graphic Artist:** Yvonne Griffith; **Photo Manager:** Les Woodrum; **Cover Designer:** Keith Blomberg; **Art Manager:** Craig Newsom; **Illustrator:** Argosy; **Printer:** United Graphics

Printed in the United States of America   10 9 8 7 6 5 4 3 2 1

Human Kinetics
Web site: www.humankinetics.com

United States: Human Kinetics, P.O. Box 5076, Champaign, IL 61825-5076
800-747-4457
e-mail: humank@hkusa.com

Canada: Human Kinetics, 475 Devonshire Road Unit 100, Windsor, ON N8Y 2L5
800-465-7301 (in Canada only)
e-mail: orders@hkcanada.com

Europe: Human Kinetics, Units C2/C3 Wira Business Park, West Park Ring Road
Leeds LS16 6EB, United Kingdom
+44 (0) 113 278 1708
e-mail: hk@hkeurope.com

Australia: Human Kinetics, 57A Price Avenue, Lower Mitcham, South Australia 5062
08 8277 1555
e-mail: liahka@senet.com.au

New Zealand: Human Kinetics, P.O. Box 105-231, Auckland Central
09-523-3462
e-mail: hkp@ihug.co.nz

contents

preface

The National Curriculum for Physical Education identifies the value of an appropriate preparation (a warm-up) for physical activity and a specific conclusion (a cool-down) to an active lesson. Yet these aspects of a professional's repertoire of teaching skills have been neglected and many teachers feel that there is an urgent need for a comprehensive update.

Jo Harris and Jill Elbourn have fulfilled this need by bringing together a whole range of suggestions that provide a host of exciting possibilities. Not only do the ideas in this book represent a comprehensive programme of suggestions that can be used within all the areas of activity identified in the National Curriculum, but these ideas can also be used in any setting (e.g., youth work or a sports club) in which people are promoting physical activity. Therefore, the principles and proposals for action identified in this book have a relevance and significance for all professionals working with young people.

The experience and expertise of the authors are considerable, and I recommend their proposals for action because they provide positive prescriptions that will enrich all work with young people.

Len Almond
Senior Lecturer, Loughborough University
October 2001

acknowledgements

The authors wish to thank Len Almond, Nick Armitage, Lorraine Cale, Sonia McGeorge, Carolyn Murphy, Mike Peyrebrune, Ian Shepherd and Pam Smith for their assistance and support in the first edition of this text.

introduction

The importance of warming up and cooling down, to prepare the body safely and effectively for exercise and to recover afterwards, is well documented. Young people need to acquire a practical knowledge and understanding of warming up and cooling down. This process starts with them following consistent good practice and culminates in them designing their own relevant and appropriate procedures.

Both in and out of school, young people should experience a variety of interesting practices that reinforce the important messages about easing into and out of exercise. This should help their exercise experiences to become more positive and comfortable, and so help to promote long-term involvement in physical activity.

This book will help you as a teacher, coach or leader to present warm-ups and cool-downs that are safe, effective, relevant, varied and enjoyable. It is also designed to help teachers guide their pupils through the progressive stages of building the necessary knowledge, understanding and skills to enable them to exercise independently once they have left school.

The book

- covers the essential theory in a straightforward manner;
- has a practical orientation;
- contains practical ideas using simple equipment; and
- is a relevant resource for primary and secondary PE teachers, students and lecturers involved in initial teacher training, sports coaches, exercise teachers and sports leaders working with children and young people.

Chapter 1 explains the requirements of the National Curriculum for Physical Education (England and Wales and the Curriculum for Northern Ireland), in terms of knowledge, skills and understanding relating to warming up and cooling down, that pupils should acquire by the end of each Key Stage. Although this book refers to the National Curriculum for England and Wales and the Curriculum for Northern Ireland, the learning outcomes are likely to be compatible with and support the curricula and sport education programmes of many other countries. Chapters 2 and 3 provide theoretical information about warming up and cooling down and answer commonly asked questions, such as "Why is a warm-up necessary?" and "For how long should cool-down stretches be held?" Chapter 4 focuses on issues associated with safe exercise practice and helps you when working with children or young people to make your own decisions about which exercises are safe, effective and appropriate. The final three chapters provide a range of practical ideas for warm-ups and cool-downs. Chapter 5 comprises ideas for working with children ages 5 to 11 (Key Stages 1 and 2), Chapter 6 focuses on ages 7 to 14 (Key Stages 2 and 3) and Chapter 7 on ages 11 to 16 (Key Stages 3 and 4).

part 1

Knowledge Base

chapter 1

National Curriculum Requirements

The National Curriculum for Physical Education for England and Wales and the Curriculum for Northern Ireland detail what pupils should know, understand and be able to do by the ages of 7, 11, 14 and 16, with specific reference to warming up and cooling down (see tables 1.1, 1.2 and 1.3).

Although this book refers to the National Curriculum for England and Wales and the Curriculum for Northern Ireland, the learning outcomes are likely to be compatible with and support the curricula and sport education programmes of many other countries.

The ultimate aim is for learners to be able to design their own warm-ups and cool-downs, and it is essential that, over time, they

1. acquire a sound knowledge base so that they understand why and how they should warm up and cool down;
2. experience a wide variety of safe, effective, relevant and enjoyable warm-ups and cool-downs across a range of activities; and
3. become progressively more involved in the learning process so that, over time, they learn how to design, carry out and evaluate warm-ups and cool-downs for themselves.

Learners' gradual move from dependence on you, the instructor (copying, following), towards independence from you (designing, evaluating) is vital to enable them to exercise by themselves safely and effectively and make judgements about good and bad practice. The combination of a sound knowledge base, positive practical experiences and increased learner involvement will assist in producing informed and

Table 1.1	National Curriculum for Physical Education (England)
Key Stage	**Requirements**
2 (ages 7-11)	Pupils should be taught to warm up and prepare appropriately for different activities.
3 (ages 11-14)	Pupils should be taught how to prepare for and recover from specific activities.
4 (ages 14-16)	Pupils should be taught how preparation, training and fitness relate to and affect performance.

Table 1.2	National Curriculum for Physical Education (Wales)
Key Stage	**Requirements**
1 (ages 5-7) **2** (ages 7-11)	Throughout the Key Stage, pupils should be taught to prepare for and recover from activity appropriately.
3 (ages 11-14)	Throughout the Key Stage, pupils should be taught relevant and safe warm-up and cool-down routines (e.g., mobility exercises, whole-body activities and static stretches) and how to take responsibility for their planning and execution.

Table 1.3	The Physical Education Curriculum (Northern Ireland)
Key Stage	**Requirements**
1 (ages 5-7)	To promote physical activity and healthy lifestyles, pupils should experience warm-up and cool-down exercises.
2 (ages 7-11)	To promote physical activity and healthy lifestyles, pupils should experience and understand the need for warm-up and cool-down exercises.
3 (ages 11-14)	To promote physical activity and healthy lifestyles, pupils should understand the appropriate warm-up and cool-down activities related to athletics, dance, games, gymnastics and swimming.
4 (ages 14-16)	Pupils should have opportunities to select and perform appropriate warm-up and cool-down activities.

independent exercisers. Increasing learner involvement implies the use of a range of teaching and learning styles. Using a range of teaching and learning styles presents learners with opportunities to become involved in decision making and to apply their knowledge and understanding to practical situations.

It is important that you carefully structure learning from the ages of 4 or 5 up to 16 to ensure clear and gradual progression of the knowledge base, practical experiences and learner involvement. Knowledge should be presented to learners in age-related and manageable sections so that they build on their understanding. The learners' practical experiences should gradually become more varied, but there should always be consistency in terms of sound philosophy and safe practice. Learner involvement should increase throughout the Key Stages to the point where they are able to work independently of you.

Table 1.4 represents the authors' interpretation of the requirements of the National Curriculum for Physical Education relating to warming up and cooling down across all Key Stages. Table 1.5 describes what the authors think learners should know, understand and be able to do by the ages of 7, 11, 14 and 16.

Table 1.4	Interpretation of the National Curriculum Requirements in Terms of Warming Up and Cooling Down
Key Stage	**Summary of what children and young people should know, understand, and be able to do by the end of each Key Stage**
1 (ages 5-7)	Pupils should know that activity starts with a gentle warm-up and finishes with a calming cool-down.
2 (ages 7-11)	Pupils should know the purpose of a warm-up and cool-down. They should recognise and describe parts of a warm-up and cool-down (i.e., exercises for the joints (e.g., arm circles), whole-body activities (e.g., jogging, skipping without a rope) and stretches for the whole body, such as reaching long and tall or parts of the body, such as the lower leg or calf muscles).
3 (ages 11-14)	Pupils should understand the value of preparing for, and recovering from, activity and the possible consequences of not doing so. They should be able to explain the purpose of, plan and perform each component of a warm-up and cool-down (i.e., mobility exercises, whole-body activities, static stretches) for general activity (e.g., games, athletics) and for a specific activity (e.g., volleyball, high jump, circuit training).
4 (ages 14-16)	Pupils should be able to evaluate warm-ups and cool-downs in terms of safety, effectiveness and relevance to the specific activity, and take responsibility for their own safe and effective preparation for, and recovery from, activity.

Table 1.5	Description of What Children and Young People Should Know, Understand and Be Able to Do By the End of Each Key Stage
Key Stage	**By the end of this Key Stage, learners should**
1 (ages 5-7)	<ul><li>know that exercise should be built up gradually and brought down gradually (similar to changing the gears of a car or bike);</li><li>be aware that a warm-up gets their body ready for exercise and a cool-down helps to slow the body down after exercise;</li><li>be aware that a warm-up should leave them feeling warm (not puffed out) and a cool-down should leave them feeling okay (not out of breath);</li><li>be able to describe and recognise actions which move their bones, activities that get their bodies warmer and actions which stretch out their whole body;</li><li>be able to follow predominantly teacher-directed warm-ups and cool-downs;</li></ul>
2 (ages 7-11)	<ul><li>understand the value of preparing the body for exercise and recovering afterwards (as in using the gears of a car or bike);</li><li>be aware that joints (where bone meets bone) have different actions (e.g., bending, straightening, turning), and that by gently moving joints the bones are helped to move more freely;</li></ul>

(continued)

Table 1.5 (continued)	Description of What Children and Young People Should Know, Understand and Be Able to Do By the End of Each Key Stage
Key Stage	**By the end of this Key Stage, learners should**
	• understand that activities which get their bodies warmer gradually raise the heart rate so that more oxygen can get to the working muscles; • be aware that they should feel warm and ready for action after a warm-up (not tired out or exhausted); • be aware that they should feel "alright" after a cool-down (not puffed out or aching); • know that muscles move bones and that stretching helps to lengthen muscles safely and prevent them from being torn or pulled; • know that they should only perform stretches when muscles are warm and that they should hold stretches still (not bounce them); • be able to demonstrate joint actions (that move bones), pulse-raising actions (that make the body warmer) and actions that stretch out the whole body and parts of the body (e.g., the back of the lower leg, the front of the upper leg, the back); • with teacher guidance be able to perform general warm-up and cool-down activities (e.g., for games activities, gymnastic activities, dance activities).
3 (ages 11-14)	• understand the need to prepare for, and recover from, exercise; know that a warm-up should contain mobility exercises (to prepare the joints), pulse-raising activities (to prepare the cardiovascular system) and gentle stretching exercises (to prepare the muscles); • know that a cool-down should contain pulse-lowering activities and longer stretches (to help prevent muscle shortening and muscle soreness); • understand that mobility exercises for the joints should be controlled within the natural range of movement of the different joints (without any flinging actions) and can be combined with pulse-raising activities; • appreciate the need for specific spinal mobility exercises for some activities; • know that pulse-raising activities should be gradually increased in intensity to about 55-60 percent of maximum heart rate or until the exercise feels quite hard or fairly hard (but not hard or very hard); • know that stretches should be static (as opposed to ballistic) and that it is only necessary to stretch out the muscles involved in the main activity (i.e., it is not necessary to stretch every muscle for every activity); • know that warm-up stretches are gentle and held for only 6-10 seconds and that cool-down stretches can be held for 10-30 seconds in comfortable, relaxed positions; • know that warm-ups and cool-downs should be directly relevant to the specific activity and can involve the use of equipment; know how to stretch specific major muscle groups safely and effectively; • be able to plan and undertake warm-ups and cool-downs suitable for specific activities (e.g., basketball, tennis, sprinting, jogging, skipping, circuit training, hockey, aerobics, rugby).
4 (ages 14-16)	• appreciate that warm-ups and cool-downs should ideally be individualised and are especially important for older people and for intense activities such as sprinting; • understand that warm-ups for activities including anaerobic work (such as games) should include faster, stronger movements following the stretches; • be able to perform combined mobility and pulse-raising activities and combined stretches (e.g., calf and chest muscles) for variety and time efficiency; • understand that certain muscle groups such as the hamstrings and groin (adductors) have a tendency to be short and tight, and would benefit from longer, relaxed stretches; • be able to design warm-ups and cool-downs for specific individuals (e.g., family members, friends, sports performers) and for specific activities (e.g., bowling, squash, fun run, sport day); • be able to perform and lead others through a wide variety of mobility, pulse-raising/pulse-lowering and stretching exercises; • be able to plan, carry out and monitor exercise programmes for themselves and others which include safe, effective, relevant and enjoyable warming up and cooling down procedures.

Warming up and cooling down also feature in the level descriptions comprising the Attainment Target within the National Curriculum for Physical Education in England and Wales. The Attainment Target describes the types and range of performance (including exceptional) that pupils working at that level should characteristically demonstrate (table 1.6).

Table 1.7 provides an example of a structured, staged approach to teaching pupils about safe and effective preparation for, and recovery from, physical activity through the areas of activity.

Teaching Warming Up and Cooling Down in the Curriculum

The process of enabling young people to become independent in terms of warming up and cooling down involves them progressively taking more prominent roles in decision making. Over a period of time, your role changes from that of leader to facilitator, which involves gradually letting go to allow the young people the freedom to think and make judgements for themselves. The way to successfully lead individuals towards independence is to involve them progressively in playing a greater role in making decisions about preparation for and recovery from activity. A sudden switch to independent decision making may be daunting for a young person, while a gradual transition helps to retain personal confidence, which is vital to independent action.

Introduce the knowledge, understanding and skills associated with preparation for and recovery from activity through the areas of activity within the curriculum. It is important to maintain pupils' interest through good planning and effective use of time. Do not view warm-ups and cool-downs as barriers to the real action, but as interesting and relevant sections of the lesson.

Table 1.6	Level Descriptions Relating to Warming Up and Cooling Down Comprising the Attainment Target		
Level	**Key Stage**	**National Curriculum for PE for England**	**National Curriculum for PE for Wales**
3	2, 3	Pupils give reasons why warming up before an activity is important and why physical activity is good for health.	
4	1, 2, 3 (expected attainment of majority of pupils aged 11)	Pupils explain and apply basic safety principles in preparing for exercise.	
5	1, 2, 3 (levels 5/6: expected attainment of majority of pupils aged 14)	Pupils warm-up and cool-down in ways that suit the activity.	Pupils perform relevant and safe warm-up and cool-down routines and begin to take some responsibility for their planning.
6	3 (levels 5/6: expected attainment of majority of pupils aged 14)	Pupils explain how to prepare for, and recover from, the activities.	Pupils take increasing responsibility for the planning and execution of safe exercises and know which exercises to avoid to prevent possible injury.

There are five main teaching guidelines for preparation for and recovery from physical activity:

1. Warm-up activities should be simple and easy to organise, as this will ensure that participants are quickly involved in activity rather than standing around listening to long explanations.

2. In cold conditions, make sure participants are active as soon as possible. Ensure that the warm-up is continuous and active by avoiding a long series of isolated mobility exercises (such as arm circles and upper-body twists) or a long series of held stretches. Instead, where possible, combine pulse-raising and mobility exercises (e.g., arm circles can be performed whilst jogging and static stretches can be interspersed with pulse raising).

3. It is good practice to allow participants to wear additional layers of clothing during the warm-up which they can remove for the main activity and replace before the cool-down.

4. Where appropriate, your active participation can be motivating for the children and can help them to gauge the pace and performance quality required.

5. In situations where class members arrive at different times, encouraging independent warm-up opportunities might ensure you involve those arriving early in preparing themselves for the main activity. Latecomers should have the opportunity to warm up before joining in the main activity.

Table 1.7	Structured, Staged Approach to Teaching Pupils About Safe and Effective Preparation for and Recovery From Physical Activity Through the Areas of Activity
Year	**Preparation for and recovery from activity** **What pupils should know or be able to do by the end of the year**
1	Activity starts with a gentle warm-up.
2	Activity finishes with a calming cool-down.
3	The purpose of a warm-up.
4	Recognise and describe parts of a warm-up (i.e., exercise for the joints (e.g., arm circles), whole-body activities (e.g., jogging, skipping without a rope) and stretches for the whole body such as reaching long and tall).
5	The purpose of a cool-down.
6	Recognise and describe parts of a cool-down (whole-body activities (e.g., walking) and stretches for the whole body or parts of the body such as the lower leg or calf muscles).
7	Understand the value of preparing for, and recovering from, activity and the possible consequences of not doing so, and be able to explain the purpose of each component of a warm-up and cool-down.
8	Plan and perform each component of a warm-up (i.e., mobility exercises, whole-body activities, static stretches) and cool-down (i.e., whole-body activities, static stretches) for general activity (e.g., athletics, dance, games).
9	Plan and perform warm-ups and cool-downs for specific activities (e.g., hockey, high jump, volleyball, circuit training).
10	Evaluate warm-ups and cool-downs in terms of safety, effectiveness and relevance to the specific activity.
11	Take responsibility for their own safe, effective and relevant preparation for and, recovery from, activity.

chapter 2

Warming Up Theory

A warm-up is a group of exercises performed immediately before activity, which helps the body to adjust from a state of rest to exercise. Warming up is an essential element of every physical education lesson or sport session to prepare the body appropriately for involvement in energetic activity. Going straight into a 100m sprint on a cold day and then collapsing onto the ground immediately afterwards is not recommended! Not only are painful muscle strains probable, but the experience is likely to be uncomfortable or even distressing. Aching muscles may be an unhappy reminder of the event for several days afterwards.

Easing into energetic exercise ensures that the exercise experience is more comfortable and that there is less likelihood of any injury. Safe involvement in enjoyable exercise is vital to promote long-term participation in physical activity. Uncomfortable and painful exercise is not likely to be repeated on a voluntary basis.

There is ongoing debate over the specific function and value of warm-ups, and whether they decrease the risk of injury. The experimental evidence is never likely to be entirely conclusive, as it would be unethical for researchers to put subjects under conditions in which they may be injured. However, the combination of evidence from research findings, together with a knowledge of muscle physiology, kinesiology and exercise psychology, tends to support the provision of a period of adjustment from rest to exercise as a prudent, protective measure for the body.

Good habits in terms of warming up should be established early in life and warming up should become an accepted element of every exercise session (whether games, gymnastics, dance, swimming, outdoor education or any other form of exercise) from a very early age.

As a physical education teacher, sports coach/leader or exercise instructor, you have an important role to play in educating people about exercise. If children are used to warming up at the start of all their lessons or sessions, they are much more likely to adopt this procedure when participating in physical activity in their own time and in adult life. In addition, they are more likely to prepare for activity by themselves if they understand the function and purpose of this procedure.

Limited time is often given as a reason for not paying sufficient attention to warm-ups. However, if you view a warm up more as a lead in activity than a separate, tagged-on section, it is far more likely to be relevant, integral and valued. Once children are able to design their own warm-ups, they can take the initiative themselves and start preparation activities whilst waiting for the whole group to assemble at the beginning of a lesson or club session.

Designing a Warm-Up

To design an effective warm-up, consider a number of factors such as length, timing and the effects a warm-up will have.

A warm-up should help participants to prepare their bodies gradually for the activity to follow. Just as it is advisable to go up through the gears in a car steadily, so it is wise to wake up the body gradually and ease it into exercise. Going straight into "fourth gear" or overdrive is likely to place undue pressure on the body and will bring about discomfort and early fatigue. A warm-up should

- prepare the mind and body for activity,
- help prevent injury, and
- help improve performance.

A warm-up comprises exercises that prepare the following body systems for activity:

1. The cardiovascular or cardiorespiratory system (heart, lungs and blood vessels)
2. The musculoskeletal system (bones, muscles, ligaments, tendons and connective tissue)
3. The neuromuscular system (the "brain-body" link)

Warm-Up Activities

Every warm-up should include

1. mobility exercises to prepare the joints (where bones join other bones);
2. pulse-raising activities to prepare the cardiovascular system (heart, lungs and blood vessels);

3. short, static stretches to prepare the muscles and their associated ligaments and connective tissue; and

4. activity-related movements to prepare the neuromuscular system (the "brain-body" link).

In addition, a warm-up should be

- active for all participants,
- relevant to the activity to follow,
- an integral part of the lesson or session, and
- varied and fun.

Use the warm-up as a valuable opportunity to recap and revise established skills and knowledge and introduce new movement ideas that can be developed later in the session. For example, a basketball lesson that focuses on dodging should include some dodging activities in the warm-up; similarly, a gymnastics lesson focusing on travelling should include numerous ways of travelling within the warm-up. In addition, warm-up activities can aid social development by incorporating the formation of groups and encouraging social interaction among individuals. Use warm-up activities to establish group sizes for later tasks, such as getting participants into threes. View the warm-up as the start of the lesson, or lead-in to the main activity, and use it to help establish the focus of the session.

Length of a Warm-Up

The length of a warm-up depends on several factors:

- The intensity of the activity to follow (i.e., how energetic it is going to be)
- The duration of the activity to follow (i.e., how long it is going to last)
- The current activity or fitness levels of the participants
- Environmental factors such as room and air temperature

The minimum length of a warm-up should be 5 to 10 minutes. Participants' getting warmer and taking off their sweatshirts or track tops is a possible indication of the effectiveness of a warm-up as it means the body temperature has been raised sufficiently. The important point is that the cardiovascular system is gradually prepared for activity. On very warm days individuals may already feel warm, but it is still important that they ease themselves into activity gradually.

Children who are less accustomed to regular exercise will probably require a slower, less intense warm-up than those who are fitter and more active. Those who are active on a regular basis will have developed more efficient response systems to the production of heat during exercise. This means that their heat-losing systems react earlier, resulting in their body tissues' requiring more intense activities or needing longer to warm up effectively. For top-class performers, before participating in major competitive events or before intensive training sessions, a warm-up may be as long as 30 to 40 minutes.

When to Warm Up

Warm-ups should immediately precede the activity to take advantage of the favourable physiological and psychological effects associated with mobility, pulse-raising and stretching exercises. When planning a lesson or club session, remember that participants should avoid sitting or standing still for too long after the warm-up or the body temperature will drop steadily and the effects of the warm-up will be reduced or lost. If instructions are necessary, give them before the warm-up or whilst participants are moving (e.g., whilst jogging on the spot) or stretching.

Effects of a Warm-Up

An effective warm-up

1. increases the heart rate and blood circulation gradually,
2. increases the body temperature,
3. permits freer movement in the joints,
4. prepares the joints and associated muscles to function through their full range of motion,
5. improves the efficiency of muscular actions,
6. reduces the risk of injury,
7. improves the transmission of nerve impulses, and
8. aids psychological preparation for the activity to follow.

Mobility Exercises

Mobility exercises move the joints (i.e., the site at which two or more bones come together, such as the shoulders, knees, hips) in a controlled manner through their normal range of movement. This helps to warm and circulate the lubricating fluid within the joints (synovial fluid), which facilitates freer movements of the joints. Synovial fluid is a thick, sticky fluid that acts as a lubricant to the joint, provides nutrient materials for the structures within the joint cavity, and helps to maintain the stability of the joint. The articular or hyaline cartilage at the ends of the bones absorbs secreted synovial fluid. This provides a smooth, sliding surface for the bones and improves the joints' shock-absorbing qualities.

There are several types of moveable joints, such as a hinge joint which allows movement in one plane only (e.g., elbow, knee) and a ball and socket joint which allows movement in all directions (e.g., shoulder, hip). You need to be familiar with the possible range of movements of each of the main joints to select a variety of exercises which mobilise them effectively. Table 2.1 describes the movements possible at each of the main joints and presents examples of mobility exercises for these joints.

Mobilising Joints Safely

Make sure mobility exercises are controlled, continuous and smooth. Avoid jerky or "flinging" movements, as these movements can damage muscles, tendons, ligaments and connective tissue by forcing them into lengthened positions at speed while they are cold.

Encourage participants to perform shoulder mobility exercises before neck mobility exercises. There is often tension in the muscles surrounding the neck, upper spine and shoulders. Release or ease this tension by performing exercises such as shoulder or arm circles before moving the small cervical vertebrae in the top part of the spine (such as neck turns or head tilts).

A warm-up should mobilise all the joints that are to be used in the main activity (usually the ankles, knees, hips, spine, shoulders, neck, elbows and wrists). Participants should perform between six and eight repetitions of each mobility exercise. Many mobility exercises can be performed whilst moving around and can be combined or interspersed with activities that raise the pulse and warm the body (walking, marching, jogging).

Pulse-Raising Activities

Pulse-raising or warming activities involve rhythmic movements of large muscle groups (particularly the major leg muscles) and bring about a gradual increase in heart rate and warm the body. Participants should start with less energetic activities and follow these with more energetic activities, for example:

- brisk walking,
- marching,

- gentle jogging,
- skipping, or
- sidestepping.

Participants should perform mobility and pulse-raising or warming exercises together. For example, walking, jogging, marching, sidestepping and knee lifts all raise the pulse and at the same time mobilise the hips, knees and ankles. Participants can mobilise the shoulder and elbow joints at the same time by adding shoulder circles or

Table 2.1	How Joints Move and How to Mobilise Them			
Joint	Type	Range of movements	Examples of mobility exercises	Teaching or coaching points
Shoulder	Ball and socket	Bending (flexion) Straightening (extending) Rotation Sideways and upwards action (abduction) Sideways and downwards action (adduction) Combination of the above (circumduction)	Shoulder or arm circles, shoulder shrugs, arm swings (forwards, backwards, across body).	Perform the exercise at a speed that can be controlled.
Neck	Pivot and hinge	Bending (flexion) Straightening (extension) Rotation	Head tilts, head turns, half circles (to the side, the front and the other side).	Perform these activities with great control. Do not force or jerk the head backwards, or forwards.
Elbow	Pivot and hinge	Bending (flexion) Straightening (extension)	Bending and straightening the elbows.	Perform movements with control. Avoid locking out the elbows when they are straight (especially if supporting body weight on your hands).
Wrist	Condyloid	Bending (flexion) Straightening (extension) Sideways and upwards action (abduction) Sideways and downwards action (adduction)	Bending and straightening the wrist, moving the wrist inwards and outwards.	Perform exercises with control.
Finger	Hinge	Bending (flexion) Straightening (extension)	Opening and closing the hand, squeezing and releasing a sponge ball.	Perform the actions with control.
Upper or middle spine	Slightly moveable	Limited bending forwards (flexion) Limited bending backwards (extension) Rotation	Upper-body twists. Curling forwards and straightening (rolling up and down through the spine).	Keep hips and kness facing forwards. Keep the knees bent to protect the lower spine. Perform the exercise with control.

(continued)

Table 2.1 (continued)	**How Joints Move and How to Mobilise Them**			
Joint	**Type**	**Range of movements**	**Examples of mobility exercises**	**Teaching or coaching points**
Lower spine	Slightly moveable	Limited bending forwards (flexion)	Side bends.	Bend directly to the side (as if between two panes of glass).
		Limited bending backwards (extension)	Hip circles.	Keep knees bent and still.
		Minimal rotation	Pelvic tilts.	Perform exercises with control.
Hip	Ball and socket	Bending (flexion) Straightening (extending) Rotation Sideways and upwards action (abduction) Sideways and downwards action (adduction) Combination of the above (circumduction)	Knee lifts, lifting knee and taking it out to the side before replacing foot on floor, marching, squats.	Keep spine tall. Perform exercises with control.
Knee	Hinge	Bending (flexion) Straightening (extension)	Squats, knee lifts, marches, most travelling actions.	Keep spine tall. Perform exercises with control.
Ankle	Hinge	Bending (flexion) Straightening (extension)	Jogging, heel-toe actions, stepping through the feet.	Do not try to rotate your ankle if it is supporting body weight.

elbow bends. Make sure participants perform pulse-raising activities for at least five minutes, depending on the intensity of the activity to follow and the environmental conditions. The function of this part of the warm-up is to go steadily "up through the gears" rather than from rest straight into energetic exercise.

Raising the Pulse Gradually

Gradually increasing intensity of the exercise raises the heart rate and breathing rate and consequently increases the supply of oxygen to the working muscles. Participants should feel warm and breathe faster but should not feel exhausted or out of breath after performing pulse-raising activities. If the exercise intensity is increased too quickly (e.g., with sprinting activities), the demands on the body systems are high and the body may have to work anaerobically (i.e., without a steady supply of oxygen).

One of the by-products of anaerobic work is lactic acid, which builds up in the muscles and leads to feelings of discomfort and fatigue. It would not be pleasant or comfortable to start an exercise session with anaerobic activities that encourage fast, strong, powerful moves such as sprint races. Avoid such activities in the early stages of a warm-up. If these activities are relevant to the main focus of the session, perform them after the body is thoroughly warm and the appropriate muscles have been stretched (e.g., towards the end of the warm-up).

Recommended Heart Rate

Pulse-raising activities should gradually raise the pulse towards the lower end of what is termed the "cardiovascular target zone". The cardiovascular target zone indicates the recommended range of heart rates for development of the cardiovascular system (heart, lungs and blood vessels). Research indicates that for adults to maintain or improve stamina or cardiovascular fitness (sometimes referred to as cardio-respiratory endurance) to enhance health, the recommended heart rate range is 55 to 90 percent of the maximum heart rate. The equivalent figures for children have yet to be determined.

Towards the end of a warm-up, it is advisable for children to have achieved heart rates of approximately 110 to 120 beats per minute.

Pulse counts are usually taken at the wrist (radial artery) or neck (carotid artery) using two fingers, or with a heart rate monitor. Pulse counting is a practised skill and may not always be appropriate or even accurate. Many factors affect heart rate, such as temperature, mood and anxiety levels. A more appropriate assessment of exercise intensity may be to ask the participants how the exercise feels. If participants describe the activities as "difficult" or "exhausting", it is likely that they are working too intensely.

Practicing Pulse-Raising Activities Safely

Use any low- to moderate-intensity activities to raise the pulse, and include a mixture of impacts. Activities can be described simply as low or high impact, depending on the forces involved in landing during the activity. For example, any activities that involve jumping up and down can be described as high impact because the entire body weight is repeatedly absorbed on landing. High-impact activities include astride jumps, jogging, jumping, skipping, leaping and galloping. Low-impact activities are those in which one foot always remains in contact with the ground (e.g., marching, brisk walking, sidestepping).

One of the health benefits of high impact exercises is that they can help to increase bone density. However, they can be strenuous, extremely energetic and can place stress on the joints. For these reasons, they are not appropriate for unfit or inactive individuals with joint problems or those who are overweight. If you select high-impact activities within a warm-up, make sure participants use the correct technique and that either you or the participant controls the level of intensity so that it remains low to moderate.

Stretches

Encourage participants to perform short stretches of the main muscles which will be involved in the activity to follow. This helps prepare these muscles to be lengthened safely and contracted vigorously and to avoid injuries, such as muscle strains. Warm-up stretches are sometimes referred to as preparatory or short stretches and are a way of signalling to the muscles that they are about to be used.

Stretching Relevant Muscles

Participants should stretch the muscles safely and slowly in a warm-up before they are lengthened at speed or contracted vigorously during the main activity. For example, the hamstrings (the muscles in the back of the upper leg) need to be stretched before taking part in a sprint event in which they will be lengthened at speed and contracted vigorously repeatedly. Examples are given in table 2.2.

Stretching also helps participants to use a greater range of movement in the activities that follow. For example, "tight" hamstring muscles will hinder a footballer or sprinter in fully extending the leg and will result in a less powerful kicking or striding action (see table 2.3).

Table 2.2	**Pulse Rate Should Reach Lower End of Target Zone at the End of a Warm-Up**
Age	**Lower end of target zone** (55-60 percent maximum heart rate; beats/15 seconds)
4-5	30-32
6-10	29-32
11-12	29-31
13-16	28-31
17-20	28-30
21-23	27-30
24-27	27-29
28-30	26-29

Table 2.3	**Muscles That Should Be Stretched After Specific Activities**
Activity	**Muscles predominantly used and which should be stretched**
Jogging	Calf muscles (back of lower leg)
Sidestepping (galloping)	Calf muscles (back of lower leg) Quadriceps (front of upper leg) Groin (inside of upper leg) Abductors (outer thigh)
Sprinting	Calf muscles (back of lower leg) Hamstrings (back of upper leg) Quadriceps (front of upper leg) Hip flexor (muscles joining top of leg to the pelvis and lower back)
Games playing (e.g., football)	Calf muscles (back of lower leg) Quadriceps (front of upper leg) Hamstrings (back of upper leg) Groin (inside of upper leg) Abductors (outer thigh)
Games playing (e.g., netball, tennis, basketball)	Calf muscles (back of lower leg) Quadriceps (front of upper leg) Hamstrings (back of upper leg) Groin (inside of upper leg) Abductors (outer thigh) Triceps (back of upper arm) Pectorals (chest) Trapezius (upper back)
Throwing and striking	Triceps (back of upper arm) Pectorals (chest) Trapezius (upper back)

When to Stretch

Ask participants to perform stretches only when muscles are warm. Warm muscles are more pliable (supple), less viscous (sticky, resistant) and can be safely lengthened without risk of injury. Cold muscles are relatively inelastic and liable to tear. A useful teaching aid to illustrate the properties of muscles is chewing gum, which tears easily when cold but becomes pliable and resistant to tearing when warm. Raised muscle temperature also helps to increase the speed of contraction and the force exerted by the muscle, while at the same time reducing viscous resistance in the connective tissue and sheathing within and around the muscle.

Safe Stretching

Passive, static stretching (in which the stretch is assisted with an external force, such as gravity or manual resistance) is the safest and most effective method of stretching muscles before exercise. Safe and effective stretching involves moving into a stretch slowly, holding it still and moving out of the stretch slowly. For most purposes, stretching the relevant muscle groups once only in a warm-up is adequate. It is more efficient and convenient to remain standing for warm-up stretches (particularly if outside on a wet, cold day). There are a variety of stretches for each major muscle group. Encourage individuals to select those stretches that best suit them and to breathe normally when stretching (some people may hold their breath while stretching).

Stretches to Avoid

Ballistic stretches (bouncing vigorously into stretches) involve repetitive contractions of the main (agonistic) muscle to stretch the opposing (antagonistic) muscle. Ballistic stretches have the potential to cause both short- and long-term damage to the muscle and often result in post-exercise muscle stiffness and soreness. This is because a vigorous bouncing action pulls on the ends of a muscle, creating microscopic muscle tears. Over time, scar tissue replaces these muscle tears, which does not have elastic properties, and reduces the muscle's overall stretch potential.

Ballistic stretching is not as effective as static stretching in lengthening a muscle. When a muscle is rapidly lengthened, a stretch reflex (or myotatic reflex) occurs which results in the same muscle contracting to avoid being damaged through overstretching. The magnitude of the muscular contraction is proportional to the speed of the stretch. This means the faster and stronger the bouncing action, the greater the muscular contraction. In effect, ballistic stretching continually triggers the stretch reflex and the muscle is constantly stretching and contracting. As a result, the muscle is never in a relaxed position so that it can lengthen safely and effectively.

Unsafe stretching techniques can cause damage to growing bones and it is especially important when working with children and young people to use slow, static stretching techniques. All children and most young people have an immature bone structure that can be easily damaged. The epiphyseal growth plates, which are composed of soft cartilagenous tissue and are situated towards the ends of the long bones, are vulnerable to the disruption that can be caused by ballistic stretching. This is because the tendon insertion, the part of the muscle which experiences the greatest amount of tension in ballistic stretching, is usually situated close to the growth plates.

Dynamic stretching may be appropriate for some high-level sport performers whose sport demands that they move into flexible positions at speed (e.g., gymnasts, trampolinists, divers, athletes and games players). If dynamic flexibility is required for high-level sport, first warm the muscles thoroughly and then perform static stretches, followed by dynamic stretches that replicate actions used within the activity or game. You will need to explain to children and young people why sport performers on television are often seen performing dynamic stretches immediately before their event. For the vast majority of the public who are exercising for health benefits, dynamic stretching is inappropriate.

Holding Stretches

Participants should move slowly into warm-up stretches and hold each still for 6 to 10 seconds. This minimises the stretch reflex and helps the muscle to relax in a gentle, lengthened position. Ask participants to take the stretch to the point at which they feel mild tension in the middle or bulky part of the muscle. If participants feel pain, advise them to ease off the stretch immediately and adopt a more comfortable position.

If participants hold the stretch for at least 6 seconds, the muscle and its supporting connective tissue have time to adapt to the lengthened position. This process of adaptation is sometimes referred to as desensitisation. Shorter, quicker stretches do not allow adequate time for such neurological adaptation to take place.

Teaching Effective Stretching

Teaching individuals to stretch effectively takes time. Participants should develop the knowledge, understanding and practical skills involved over a number of years. For a stretch to be effective, it needs to be performed well. Participants should know which muscle they are stretching and understand why the stretch is necessary.

Clearly indicate to participants where they should feel the stretch. Encourage participants to relax when stretching and never force muscles into lengthened positions. Typical teaching points and useful phrases for teaching stretches include:

- ease into the stretch slowly,
- hold the stretch still; do not bounce,
- feel mild tension in the middle of the stretched muscle,
- if you feel any pain or the muscle starts shaking, ease off the stretch immediately,
- relax all other parts of your body, particularly your head, shoulders and back,
- don't fight against the muscle; try and relax,
- if comfortable and the muscle feels relaxed, try increasing the stretch gently and holding the new position still, and
- gently ease out of the stretch.

Planning sequences of stretches that permit easy transitions from one position to the next helps flow and continuity and is particularly time efficient. When individuals are familiar with correct stretching positions and procedures, combine upper-body and lower-body stretches. For example, combine calf stretches with stretches for the chest (pectorals), triceps (back of upper arm), shoulder muscles (deltoids) or upper back muscles (trapezius and rhomboids). It is important to introduce combined stretches only when participants have good body awareness and perform isolated stretches with the correct technique. When teaching or performing combined stretches, encourage participants to take up the lower-body stretch first and, once they have established a firm stable base, assume the upper-body stretch.

Keeping Warm While Stretching

As stretching is static, intersperse stretches with pulse-raising activities so that individuals stay warm. Performing a long, continuous series of static stretches outside on a cold day is not advisable. Ask participants to perform a couple of stretches followed by some pulse-raising activities, and then some more stretches. Once individuals are familiar with upper-body stretches, they can perform them whilst walking, jogging, sidestepping or marching. This helps to maintain body temperature and adds variety to the warm-up procedures.

Teaching Stretching Early

There is little evidence to suggest that younger children frequently pull muscles during activity. However, it is important that good habits be established early on in life and that individuals learn at an early age that stretching is an important part of activity preparation and recovery. The knowledge, understanding and skills relating to stretching need to be developed in a progressive manner. The stretches considered appropriate for the four National Curriculum Key Stages are presented in table 2.4. Table 2.5 provides a summary of the location, action and recommended stretches (with teaching or coaching points) for the major muscle groups.

Table 2.4	Recommended Stretches for Each Key Stage
Key Stage	**Recommended stretches**
1 (ages 4-7)	Whole-body stretches: standing, sitting, lying down
2 (ages 7-11)	Stretches for parts of the body; for example, arms, middle, back Stretches for specific major muscles; for example, back of lower leg, front of upper leg, back of upper leg, inside of upper leg, chest
3 (ages 11-14)	Key Stage 2 stretches plus stretches for all the major muscle groups, including some partner stretches
4 (ages 14-16)	Key Stages 2 and 3 stretches plus a variety of stretches for all the major muscles, including some combined stretches

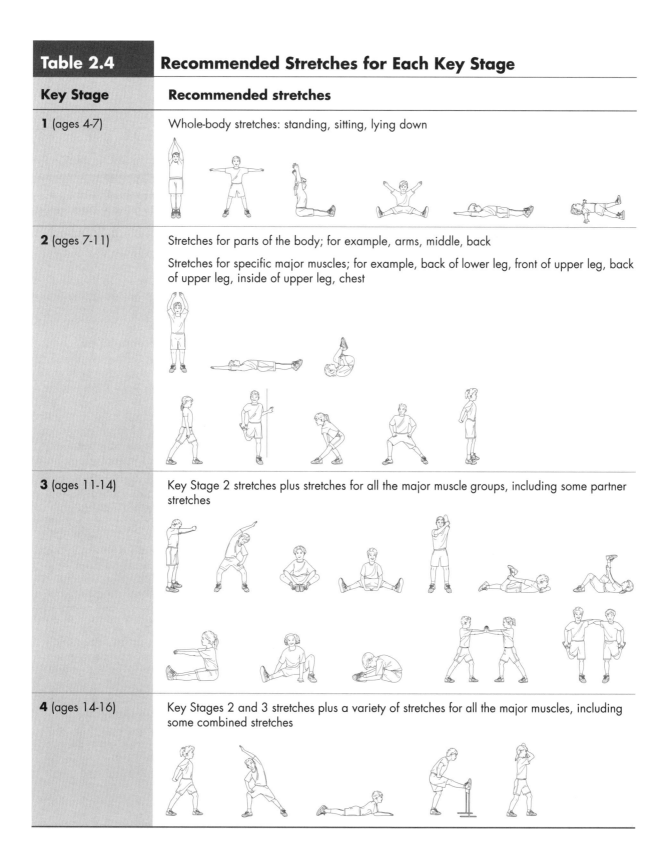

Table 2.5	Muscles—Location, Action and Recommended Stretches		
Muscle group and location	**Muscle action**	**How to stretch it**	**Main teaching or coaching points**
Gastrocnemius Upper calf muscle Back of lower leg	Raises the heel and bends the knee (e.g., in walking, jogging, running, and skipping).		Toes pointing forwards. Back leg straight, heel down. Back straight.
Soleus Bottom calf muscle Back of lower leg	Raises the heel (e.g., in walking, jogging, running, and skipping).		Toes pointing forwards. Both legs bent. Tuck pelvis under. Weight mainly on back leg. Back straight.
Quadriceps Front of upper leg	Extends (straightens) the knee (e.g., in jumping, running, lunges, step-ups).		Keep your supporting knee slightly bent, push your hip forward and your shoe or foot back against your hand, keep your knees close together.
Hamstrings Back of upper leg	Bends the knee (e.g., in kicking, leg curls, lifting heel to backside).		Standing—keep your tummy pulled tight and your back straight, hands on your hips or at the top of the bent leg, look forwards, tilt the backside upwards. Lying—keep head and shoulders on the floor, bend the leg which you are not stretching, ease thigh towards chest.
Adductors Inner thigh or groin	Brings the leg inwards towards the centre line of the body (e.g., jumping feet together when performing astride jumps).		Standing—keep your hips and shoulders facing forwards, keep the knee of the bent leg at 90°. Standing and sitting—keep your back tall and straight.
Iliopsoas Hip flexor	Flexion (bending) at the hips (e.g., as in knee lifts, marching, stepping, squats).		Keep your front knee at 90°, press your hip forwards, keep your back tall and straight.
Abductors Outer thigh muscles	Lifts the leg sideways and away from the body (e.g., jumping with feet apart in astride jumps).		Sitting—back straight and tall, bring knee towards opposite shoulder. Lying—keep your head and shoulders on the floor, ease your thigh towards your chest.
Rectus abdominis Straight abdominal muscles	Supports and flexes the spine (bend forwards) (e.g., curl-ups, bending).		Keep forearms on the floor to avoid overarching (hyperextending) the spine, press rib cage along floor and lift gently.

Table 2.5 (continued)	Muscles—Location, Action and Recommended Stretches		
Muscle group and location	**Muscle action**	**How to stretch it**	**Main teaching or coaching points**
Obliques Side abdominal muscles	Supports and rotates the spine (bend forwards and twist) (e.g., twisting curl-ups).		Lying—keep head and shoulder on the floor, heel and knees together, "look" the opposite way from your knees. Standing—keep your knees slightly bent, reach upwards and directly over.
Gluteus maximus Backside muscles (bottom)	Extends (straightens) the hip (e.g., standing up from squats or lunges or lifting a straight leg behind when lying or standing).		Keep head and shoulders on the floor, hug knees into your chest (hands under knees).
Erector spinae Muscles along length of spine	Supports and extends (arches) the spine (e.g., back raises).		Try to touch knees with nose, hold the curled position still, hug your knees into your chest (hands under knees).
Trapezius Across the upper back	Brings the shoulder blades towards the mid-line of the spine (e.g., shoulder squeezes).		Keep your elbows slightly bent, round the spine, lower your chin towards your chest.
Pectorals Chest muscles	Horizontal flexion, adduction and inwards rotation of the shoulder (e.g., chest pass, hitting a forehand in tennis, throwing a discus).		Keep spine tall and straight, pull tummy tight, squeeze your shoulder blades together.
Deltoids Front, top and back of shoulders	Lifts arm forwards and up-wards (flexion of shoulder); outwards and upwards (abduction of shoulder) and backwards and upwards (extension of shoulder) (e.g., lifting arms to the side, forwards and behind).		Keep spine tall and straight, pull tummy tight, squeeze your shoulder blades together. Keep your elbows slightly bent, round the spine, lower your chin towards your chest.
Triceps Back of upper arm	Extends (straightens) elbow (e.g., as in throwing and doing push-ups).		Look ahead and keep neck relaxed, use your other arm in front or above elbow to assist.

End of a Warm-Up

After a warm-up, individuals (see table 2.6) should feel

- OK,
- comfortable,
- warm,
- ready for action,
- a little bit puffed,
- good,
- alert, and
- ready for more exercise.

Participants should not feel worn out, out of breath or fit to drop.

Table 2.6	Summary of Components of a Warm-Up	
Component	**Purpose of component**	**Alternative terms**
Mobilising or loosening up	To prepare the joints for further activity by moving them in a controlled manner to warm and circulate synovial fluid, which permits freer, easier movement.	Getting the joints ready for action. Oiling the joints. Loosening up.
Pulse raising or warming	To prepare the cardiovascular system (heart, lungs, and blood vessels) for further activity by gently raising the intensity of the exercise, which brings about a gradual increase in breathing rate and heart rate.	Getting warm. Warming the muscles. Taking the body up through the gears. Preparing the heart, lungs and blood vessels for activity.
Stretching	To prepare the muscles for further activity by gently lengthening them statically. This prepares the muscles for being lengthened or contracted at speed in the main activity and helps to prevent unnecessary muscle tears.	Lengthening the muscles. Stretching out.

chapter 3

Cooling Down Theory

A cool-down or warm-down is a group of exercises performed immediately after activity that provides the body with a period of adjustment from exercise to rest. Cooling down is an essential element of every physical education lesson or sports session in order to help the body to recover safely and effectively from energetic activity. Going straight from "fifth" to "first gear" can be an uncomfortable experience and a cool-down is especially important after intense exercise to help combat problems such as dizziness, fainting and nausea, which may occur if a gradual easing off process is not followed.

Recovering gradually from energetic exercise is more comfortable and there is less likelihood of post-exercise stiffness and soreness. Safe involvement in enjoyable exercise is vital to promote long-term participation in physical activity. Uncomfortable and painful exercise is not likely to be repeated on a voluntary basis.

There is ongoing debate over the specific function and value of cool-downs. The experimental evidence is never likely to be entirely conclusive, as it would be unethical for researchers to put subjects under conditions in which they may be injured. However, the combination of evidence from research findings, together with a knowledge of muscle physiology, kinesiology and exercise psychology, tends to support the provision of a period of adjustment from exercise to rest as a prudent, protective measure for the body.

Good habits in terms of cooling down should be established early in life and cooling down should become an accepted element of every physical education lesson or club session (whether games, gymnastics, dance, swimming, outdoor education or any other form of exercise) from a very early age.

As a physical education teacher, sports coach/leader or exercise instructor, you have an important role to play in educating people about exercise. If children are used to cooling down at the end of all their lessons or sessions, they are much more likely to adopt this procedure when participating in physical activity in their own time and in adult life. In addition, they are more likely to cool down by themselves if they understand the function and purpose of this procedure.

Limited time is often given as a reason for not paying sufficient attention to cool-downs. However, if you view the cool-down more as a concluding activity than a separate, tagged-on section, it is far more likely to be relevant, integral and valued. Once children are able to design their own cool-downs, they can take the initiative themselves.

Designing a Cool-Down

To design an effective cool-down, consider a number of factors such as length, timing and the effects a cool-down will have. A cool-down should help participants to prepare their bodies gradually to stop exercising. Just as it is advisable to change down steadily through the gears of a car, so it is wise to ease the body gradually out of exercise. Going straight from "fourth gear" to inactivity may result in dizziness, fainting or nausea.

A cool-down should

- prepare the body to stop exercising,
- help prevent unnecessary post-exercise muscle stiffness and soreness, and
- return the body gradually to a pre-exercise condition.

A cool-down comprises exercises that help the following body systems to recover from energetic activity:

1. the cardiovascular or cardiorespiratory system (heart, lungs and blood vessels)
2. the musculoskeletal system (bones, muscles, ligaments, tendons and connective tissue)
3. the neuromuscular system (the "brain-body" link).

Cool-Down Activities

Every cool-down should include:

1. pulse-lowering activities, which prepare the cardiovascular system (heart, lungs and blood vessels) safely and gradually to slow down and stop exercising; and
2. static stretching exercises to maintain or develop flexibility in the muscle groups used in the previous activity.

In addition, a cool-down should be

- active for all participants,
- relevant to the previous activity, and
- an integral part of the lesson or session.

Use the cool-down as a valuable opportunity to recap and summarise the main focus of the session. View the cool-down as a part of the session and use it effectively as a relevant conclusion. For example, a dance session which focuses on learning and performing a motif could end with participants performing the motif using slow and controlled movements; similarly, a games session which focuses on one-to-one marking could end with "follow-my-leader" activities which gradually decrease in intensity.

Length of a Cool-Down

The length of a cool-down depends on several factors:

- The intensity of the previous activity (how energetic it was);
- The duration of the previous activity (how long it lasted); and
- The current fitness or activity levels of the participants.

The minimum length of a cool-down should be three to five minutes. Participants breathing normally and feeling "OK" are possible indications of the effectiveness of a cool-down. The important point is that the cardiovascular system recovers gradually after activity.

Children who are less accustomed to regular exercise will probably require a longer, more gradual cool-down than those who are fitter and more active. Those who are more active on a regular basis will recover more quickly after energetic exercise. For top-class performers after participating in major competitive events or after intensive training sessions a cool-down may be as long as 10 to 15 minutes.

When to Cool-Down

Cool-downs should immediately follow energetic activity whilst the major muscle groups are warm. When planning a lesson or club session, remember that participants should avoid sitting or standing still for too long after the main activity or the body temperature will drop rapidly (especially on a cold day) and the muscles will be too cold to stretch effectively. If a summary or questions are necessary, include them after the cool-down or whilst participants are moving (e.g., whilst jogging on the spot) or stretching.

Effects of a Cool-Down

An effective cool-down

1. decreases the heart rate and blood circulation gradually;
2. aids venous return (by keeping the leg muscles contracting to help avoid blood pooling in the legs and to assist the return of blood to the heart);
3. assists in the removal of waste products (particularly lactic acid, which may have built up as a by-product of vigorous anaerobic work such as sprinting or jumping), allowing a quicker and more comfortable recovery from exercise;
4. helps to maintain or develop flexibility in muscles that have been continually shortened or are tight;
5. helps to minimise post-exercise muscle stiffness and soreness;
6. releases unnecessary tension and assists relaxation; and
7. returns the body safely and effectively to a pre-exercise condition.

Pulse-Lowering Activities

Pulse-lowering activities involve rhythmic movements of the large muscle groups (particularly the major leg muscles) and bring about a gradual decrease in heart rate. The intensity of these movements should be gradually decreased. Participants should start with more energetic activities and follow these with less energetic activities, for example:

- fast running,
- vigorous marching,
- gentle jogging,
- brisk walking and
- steady-paced walking.

The function of this part of the cool-down is to take the body steadily "down through the gears", rather than stop suddenly after energetic exercise (see table 3.1, p. 29). Make sure participants perform pulse-lowering activities for approximately one to three minutes or longer, depending on the intensity and duration of the previous activity. If the main activity did not include fast, vigorous exercise, it may not be necessary to perform pulse-lowering exercises. Very often, the walk or jog from the courts or pitches back to the changing rooms keeps the main leg muscles moving, which assists the blood circulation and disperses any small amounts of lactic acid built up in the muscles. For example, after a hockey, rugby or soccer session, ask participants to jog half way back to the changing rooms, to walk the rest of the way and to stretch out the major leg muscles before they go indoors. This is good practice as it incorporates pulse lowering and stretching of the main muscle groups involved in the previous activity.

Lowering the Pulse Gradually

Gradually decreasing the intensity of the exercise lowers the heart and breathing rates. Participants should feel that their breathing and heart rate have recovered to pre-exercise levels and should not feel exhausted or out of breath. If the previous activity involved powerful, vigorous exercise such as fast sprinting or jumping which resulted in participants being out of breath, the leg muscles will have accumulated lactic acid as a by-product of the anaerobic work (i.e., the body having to produce energy in the absence of a steady supply of oxygen). Keeping the legs moving assists lactic acid dispersal and the action of the leg muscles will help to pump blood back to the heart.

Standing still or sitting down after an energetic bout of exercise (such as a 100m sprint race) results in blood pooling in the leg muscles as well as an accumulation of lactic acid. This leads to feelings of discomfort and pain and participants may feel light-headed or faint because of a reduction in the supply of blood and oxygen to the heart and brain. The body's response to this is dizziness and possibly fainting as it tries to restore an adequate blood flow to these essential organs. Encourage participants to remain on their feet and to keep moving around (walking, gentle jogging, light marching) until they are no longer out of breath, feel normal and their legs no longer feel heavy.

In an exercise session, the upper body, rather than the leg muscles, may have worked hard. For example, if the session includes numerous push-ups, participants will need to keep the muscles in the back of their arms and chest moving to disperse any buildup of lactic acid. Participants can do this through simple mobility exercises involving bending and straightening the arms. The key is to keep moving the muscles that have just performed fast, energetic actions.

Recommended Heart Rate

Pulse-lowering activities should gradually lower the pulse back to about 55 to 60 percent of maximum heart rate or lower. Towards the end of a cool-down, it is advisable for children to have reduced their heart rates to at least 110 to 120 beats per minute. For further information about how to monitor the heart rate see "Recommended Heart Rate" in chapter 2 on page 15.

Stretches

Encourage participants to perform stretches for the main muscles worked on in the session. This helps to return these muscles to their pre-exercise or resting length (see table 3.1 on page 29). Stretches performed for this purpose are referred to as maintenance stretches. The cool-down is also an ideal time to develop flexibility (range of movement around joints) as the muscles are thoroughly warmed and can be lengthened safely. Stretches performed for this purpose are referred to as developmental stretches.

Stretching Relevant Muscles

Participants should stretch out the muscles that have been working in the preceding activity. For example, after jogging or skipping, participants need to stretch out the calf muscles (both the gastrocnemius and the soleus muscles) to avoid them remaining in a contracted, shortened position. After sprinting, participants should thoroughly stretch the hamstrings (back of upper leg muscles), quadriceps (front of upper leg muscles), groin (inside of upper leg or adductors) and calf muscles (back of lower leg). After gymnastics focusing on supporting body weight, participants should stretch muscles in the shoulders (deltoids), triceps (back of upper arm) and chest (pectorals). Examples are presented in table 2.3.

Some muscle groups tend to be tight or short as a result of everyday actions such as many hours of sitting down or as a result of repetitive sporting actions, such as kicking a ball. Most individuals find that hamstrings (back of the upper leg) and the groin or adductors (inside of the thigh) tend to be tight. Tight muscles restrict potential range of movement and, in the case of short hamstrings, can adversely affect posture. For these reasons, it is important to develop the length of these muscles by holding them in comfortable, relaxed, stretched positions. Progress the duration of the stretch over time, and encourage individuals to move slowly into the stretch and to gently apply a little more pressure to the stretch when they feel the muscle relaxing.

When to Stretch

Participants should perform cool-down stretches only when muscles are very warm. For more information about why it is important to perform stretches only when muscles are warm see chapter 2, "When to Stretch", page 17.

Safe Stretching

Passive, static stretching (in which the stretch is assisted with an external force such as gravity or manual resistance) is recommended. Research has demonstrated that static, long duration stretches performed when the muscle temperature is elevated are effective for lengthening muscles. Participants should relax and move slowly into each stretch until they feel mild tension (but no pain) in the bulky part of the muscle. If participants feel any pain or discomfort, they should ease the stretch immediately until they find a comfortable position. Participants should not try to compete with each other. Stretching is a very personal and individual process and should be respected as such. For further information about safe stretching, see chapter 2's "Safe Stretching" and "Stretches to Avoid" sections on page 17.

Holding Stretches

Maintenance stretches (to return muscles to pre-exercise length) should be performed after every activity session and held still for 10 to 20 seconds. Research indicates that developmental stretches (to increase flexibility) should be performed as many as three or four times, held for up to 60 seconds each time and performed as frequently as twice a day. Given the time constraints in most lessons and club sessions, there may only be time to perform each developmental stretch once and to hold each for between 10 and 30 seconds. Encourage individuals wanting or needing significant improvements in flexibility to perform stretching exercises every other day or, better still, daily as part of a planned flexibility programme.

If participants perform several or a series of stretches in the cool-down, plan the stretching sequence so that there is continuity and it flows smoothly. Not only does continuity and flow help to promote a calm, relaxed atmosphere conducive to a cool-down but it is also much more time efficient. If individuals become accustomed to a particular stretching sequence, they are less likely to overlook any important stretches. For more information about teaching effective stretching and ensuring that stretches are developmentally appropriate, see section "Teaching Effective Stretching" in chapter 2, page 18.

Keeping Warm While Stretching

As the body temperature decreases gradually during the cool-down, advise participants to replace outer layers of clothing (e.g., tracksuit tops, sweatshirts, jogging bottoms) as soon as possible to avoid feeling cold. Stretching exercises in the cool-down are most effectively performed in comfortable, relaxed positions. Where appropriate and convenient, this may involve taking the body to the floor or ground or onto a mat. This will not be possible or desirable outside on a wet, windy, cold day. Outside, participants can perform stretches in a standing position, either unsupported or with the support of a partner, wall or tree.

PNF Stretching

Proprioceptive neuromuscular facilitation (PNF) is considered to be an advanced form of stretching which takes advantage of the reflex action which occurs within a highly tensed muscle causing it to relax. This response to a prolonged, strong increase in muscle length or muscle contraction is sometimes referred to as

- the inverse stretch (or myotatic) reflex,
- the Golgi tendon organ response (GTOs are sense organs or proprioceptors found at the end of muscle fibres or tendons) or
- autogenic inhibition.

This relaxation response to muscle tension, which can be built up either during a long held stretch or during a strong muscle contraction, is a protective mechanism to prevent injury to tendons and muscles.

For high-level sports performers and dancers who are serious about increasing their flexibility, PNF is a most effective form of stretching. However, PNF stretching requires a mature, responsible and informed approach to planned and controlled exercise. If performed inappropriately or without proper instruction, PNF stretches can cause serious injury.

End of a Cool-Down

After a cool-down individuals should feel

- OK,
- comfortable,
- normal,
- good,
- alright and
- relaxed.

Table 3.1	Summary of Components of a Cool-Down	
Component	**Purpose of component**	**Alternative terms**
Pulse-lowering or cooling activities	To prepare the cardiovascular system (heart, lungs, and blood vessels) to stop exercising by gradually lowering the intensity of the exercise, which brings about a gradual decrease in breathing and heart rate. After vigorous exercise, movement of the large muscles helps to speed up recovery by dispersing any lactic acid built up in the muscles and by assisting the veins in pumping the blood back to the heart.	Cooling off Easing down Taking the body down through the gears Calming down the body and brain
Stretching exercises	To maintain or develop flexibility in the muscles which have been continuously contracted in the main activity. This should help prevent unnecessary stiffness and soreness caused by muscle shortening and should help to keep a good range of movement about the joints.	Lengthening the muscles Stretching out

Relaxation

If there is enough time, participants might appreciate a focus on relaxation after a vigorous exercise session. The cool-down is a suitable time for this, as individuals are winding while they are performing stretches in comfortable positions.

Formal relaxation sessions do not appeal to everyone, and teachers and coaches will need to judge how individuals are likely to react and cope with a specific focus on relaxation. Many teachers and coaches have been pleasantly surprised by the positive reaction of groups to this area of work.

A number of relaxation methods are possible. The simplest method is to give participants a minute or two to themselves after their stretches to relax in any comfortable position and "switch off" from everything. Encourage individuals to close their eyes and help them to relax by asking them to focus on slow, controlled breathing and releasing muscle tension. Appropriate, relaxing music may help this process. Use several relaxation techniques, such as tensing and relaxing muscles, pressing into the floor and then releasing, or encouraging a sinking, heavy feeling as participants slowly breathe out, allowing the floor (or chair) to increasingly support body weight.

If teachers include two or three minutes or more of relaxation within a lesson or exercise session, they should wake up participants' body systems again, rather than shock them back into reality by jumping up quickly and rushing to get changed. Once participants have slowly gotten to their feet (and they may need to be talked through this to ensure that it is gradual), performing some low-intensity, easy, rhythmic exercises (e.g., shaking out the arms and legs, low marching) will promote the circulation and prepare them for whatever follows (e.g., another lesson or a journey home).

Minimising Stiffness and Soreness

The day after an exercise session (or several days later), many people experience stiffness and soreness in their muscles. This is referred to as DOMS (delayed onset muscular soreness). Several factors are considered to contribute towards DOMS, including ballistic exercises (which cause miniscule muscle tears), excessive unfamiliar work (particularly associated with eccentric contractions, that is contractions in which the muscle is lengthening), accumulation of lactic acid and tight, short muscles after repeated muscular contractions.

An adequate cool-down will not guarantee avoiding post-exercise soreness but should help to minimise it by dissipating lactic acid effectively and maintaining and developing flexibility in shortened muscles. Table 3.2 summarises the effects of warming up and cooling down. Hot showers, baths or massage may also aid recovery after a particularly strenuous bout of exercise.

Table 3.2	Summary of the Effects of Warming Up and Cooling Down	
	Warming up	**Cooling down**
Breathing rate	Gradually increases	Gradually decreases
Body temperature	Gradually increases	Gradually decreases
Heart rate	Gradually increases	Gradually decreases
Blood vessel diameter	Dilates (increases)	Constricts (decreases)
Oxygen exchange and delivery	Gradually increases	Gradually decreases
Rate of metabolic process	Gradually increases	Gradually decreases
Muscle temperature	Gradually increases	Gradually decreases
Muscle elasticity	Gradually decreases	Gradually decreases
Muscle viscosity (resistance)	Gradually decreases	Gradually increases
Joint lubrication	Gradually increases	Gradually decreases
Neuromuscular links	Gradually increase	Gradually decrease

chapter 4

Safe, Appropriate and Effective Exercise

Many exercises commonly performed in the past are now considered to be potentially harmful if used on a regular basis (e.g., the "hurdles" stretch, "windmills", full head circling, standing straight leg toe touch). As a teacher, coach or leader, you may frequently be asked questions about whether specific exercises are appropriate for children and young people. This chapter provides information to help you conduct risk assessments and make your own decision about which exercises are safe, effective and appropriate when working with children or young people. For the purposes of this chapter, those aged approximately 5 to 10 years are referred to as children and those aged 11 to 18 as young people.

Safe Exercises

Evaluate each exercise in relation to the following issues:

- **Alignment.** Does the exercise place or move joints in alignment (i.e., in anatomically correct ways)? Table 4.1 focuses on safety issues associated with alignment.
- **Impact.** Have the risks associated with high-impact activities been minimised? Table 4.2 focuses on safety issues associated with impact.
- **Momentum.** Can the exercise be performed in a controlled manner? Table 4.3 focuses on safety issues associated with momentum.

If the answer to each of the above questions is "yes", then consider the exercise to be safe.

Table 4.1 Safety Issues Associated With Alignment

Description	Examples of unsafe practice	Risk implications for children and young people	Recommendations for minimising risk	Examples of safe practice
Placing joints in anatomically correct positions or moving joints in anatomically correct ways.	*Knees:* performing weight-bearing or jumping activities with deep knee bends (e.g., bunny jumps, burpees). Hurdles stretch. Performing any activity with knees knocking inwards (e.g., astride jumps, jogging). *Spine:* hyperflexion of the spine (e.g., standing straight leg toe touch, feet touching ground behind head when lying on back). Hyperextension of the spine (e.g., bridge position, neck circling). Activities which attempt to rotate the lumbar region of the spine (e.g., windmills).	Any exercise that is performed with poor alignment may strain ligaments and tendons. Ligament and tendon insertions are often situated near the weak epiphyseal growth plates at the ends of the bones. Repetitive strain on tendons and ligaments during periods of growth may lead to joint laxity (instability). Hyperflexion and hyperextension of the spine may result (over a long period of time) in displacement of discs, which can lead to back pain and restricted movement.	Ensure that joints are moved and placed in anatomically correct positions. Teachers need to know and understand the range of motion about the joints moving. Teachers should use teaching points and demonstrations to help children and young people perform exercises with correct alignment. Children and young people should understand the safety issues associated with joint alignment and know how to check their own and others' exercise technique. Exercises that do not place or move joints in alignment should be adjusted (in terms of technique) or substituted for safer alternatives.	Correct knee alignment: knees over toes (e.g., knee bends, squats, astride jumps, standing adductor (inner thigh) stretch). Correct alignment of spine: tall spine, tummy pulled through to backbone (e.g., posture in warm up exercises, squats, hamstring stretch). Upper-body twists to mobilise thoracic area of spine.

Table 4.2	Safety Issues Associated With Impact			
Description	Examples of unsafe practice	Risk implications for children and young people	Recommendations for minimising risk	Examples of safe practice
Impact refers to force exerted against the floor. A high-impact activity is one that involves a great amount of force acting against the floor, as in landing from a jump. It is an over-simplification to suggest that activities that involve jumping are all high impact (e.g., if skipping and jogging are performed efficiently, using protective footwear and on suitable surfaces (sprung floor or grass), it may be possible to decrease the intensity of the impact). High-impact, weight-bearing activities stimulate healthy bone growth and development. A low-impact activity is one that involves a small amount of force acting against the floor, as in walking.	Warm-ups comprising only high-impact activities performed on the spot (e.g., astride jumps, skipping, jogging), particularly when performed with poor technique on hard surfaces and without supportive footwear.	Excessive exposure to high-impact activities may lead to the development of shin splints, tendonitis, and tibial and fibial stress fractures. An even higher risk of injury may result if these activities are performed with poor technique, unsupportive footwear, or on hard floors. High-impact activities tend to be high intensity. The anaerobic threshold of young people is lower than that of adults and their potential to perform intense, explosive activities is not as great as adults. In addition, because they do not perceive exercise at a given intensity to be as strenuous as adults, they might continue to work when they are already fatigued.	Young people need to understand the benefits and risks associated with performing high-impact activities. Teachers should ensure that when young people are involved in high-impact activities, they • wear supportive footwear; take off and land with safe technique; • alternate high- and low-impact activities; • perform high-impact activities on resilient surfaces whenever possible (e.g., sprung floors or grass); • do not perform excessive amounts of high-impact activity.	Alternating high- and low-impact activities (e.g., brisk walking and astride jumps; stepping using a bench and jogging; knee lifts and skipping without a rope).

Table 4.3		Safety Issues Associated With Momentum		
Description	**Examples of unsafe practice**	**Risk implications for children and young people**	**Recommendations for minimising risk**	**Examples of safe practice**
Performing exercises or activities in an uncontrolled manner.	In a warm-up or cool-down: • flinging arms when performing mobility exercises for the shoulders; • performing upper-body twists and side bends with momentum; • uncontrolled bouncing into stretches at the end of their range.	Warm-up exercises performed using flinging or momentum or uncontrolled bouncing into stretches. These take the muscles to the end of their range at speed, while they are cold and at their least pliable. This may result in muscle tears or injury to the tendon or tendon insertion. In young people tendon insertions are often situated close to the vulnerable epiphyseal growth plates. Young people may have tight and relatively weak muscles following a growth spurt. Weak, tight muscles may be particularly susceptible to injury caused by performing exercises with momentum (e.g., uncontrolled bouncing into stretches may cause minute or more acute muscle tears which can lead to stiffness, soreness, and decreased pliability).	Ensure that all warm-up exercises are performed in a controlled manner. Teachers should not expect all young people to achieve the same range of motion about joints: they should allow for those with tight and weak muscles and provide alternatives for performing exercises that are appropriate for individuals. Warm-up and cool-down stretches should be performed statically and with safe and effective technique.	"Placing the arms" during swinging or circling mobility exercises in warm-up. Warm-up and cool-down stretches held still and performed with joints in alignment.

Appropriate Exercises

To assess the risk factors associated with children or young people performing particular exercises, you need to

- know the purpose of a range of exercises,
- know and understand the physiological issues which might affect a child's or young person's response to exercise (see table 4.4), and
- understand the principles of safe exercise practice in terms of alignment, impact and momentum (see tables 4.1, 4.2 and 4.3).

Effective Exercises

To evaluate whether an exercise is effective, ask the following questions:

- What is the purpose of the exercise?
- Does the exercise fulfil its purpose?

Table 4.4	How Children and Young People Respond to Exercise	
Issue	**Risk factors**	**Recommendations for minimising risk**
Children cannot regulate their body temperature as efficiently as adults. They have a • lower rate of sweat production, • higher rate of heat production, • higher ratio of body surface to weight than adults.	Children heat up rapidly during exercise and overheat easily in hot weather. Children lose heat rapidly in cold weather or conditions.	In hot weather encourage children to wear light clothing, reduce exercise intensity, take frequent rest periods and have plenty of fluids available. In cold weather or conditions ensure that children are wearing sufficient clothing to conserve body heat (in very cold conditions this may include hats and gloves) and that activity levels are high (a short, high-activity session is preferable to a longer, less active session).
Children's bones are weaker than adults'. In children and young people bone growth occurs in the cartilage of the epiphyseal plates in the long bones.	Growth plates are vulnerable to injury because they are 2-5 times weaker than the ligaments. Injury to growth plates is rare but can be caused by repetitive compressive loads (e.g., in wrists and elbows of gymnasts) and can lead to permanent damage to growing bones.	Encourage children and young people to take part in a variety of activities and discourage them from excessive participation in one sport or activity, especially if they are doing it every day and starting to look tired.
Following a growth spurt, a young person's muscles will be relatively thin, weak, and tight. The adolescent growth spurt can lead to height changes of up to six inches in just over two years.	Immediately after a period of rapid growth, many young people will experience muscle tightness which may result in • restricted range of movement around some joints, and • an imbalance between flexibility and strength in opposing muscles, which may result in poor joint alignment and a higher risk of injury.	During periods of active growth ensure that young people are encouraged and helped to • develop flexibility and muscular strength in the main muscle groups to reduce muscle tightness, avoid muscle imbalance and maintain a good range of movement about joints, • perform exercises with correct alignment of joints.

To determine whether an exercise fulfils its purpose, you need a basic knowledge (see table 4.5) of

- anatomy and physiology, and
- which exercises are suitable for inclusion in a warm-up and cool-down.

Exercise Risk Assessment

Every exercise comprises both *benefits* and *costs:*

- To identify benefits, consider the purpose of an exercise and whether the exercise fulfils its purpose.
- To identify costs, consider if the exercise is appropriate for the person performing it and the safety of the exercise (with respect to alignment, impact and momentum).

To carry out a risk assessment, identify both the *benefits* and the *costs* incurred in performing a specific exercise and then weigh these up to determine the level of risk. If

Table 4.5	Warming Up and Cooling Down—Essential Knowledge for Teachers
Type of exercise	**What teachers need to know**
Mobility exercises	The purpose of mobility exercises (see pp. 12, 13-14, 22).
	The possible range of motion about the major joints (see pp. 12-14).
Pulse-raising or -lowering exercises	The purpose of pulse-raising or -lowering exercises (see pp. 22, 23).
	How to increase or decrease exercise intensity in a gradual manner (e.g., by enlarging or reducing the speed and size of movements).
Warm-up or cool-down stretches	The purpose of warm-up or cool-down stretches (see pp. 9-10, 22, 23-24, 29).
	The location and insertions of the major muscle groups (see pp. 20-21).

the *costs* of performing a specific exercise outweigh or equal the *benefits* (figure 4.1), the exercise is high risk and you should not ask learners to perform it. Substitute any high-risk activity for a low-risk alternative which provides the same or similar benefits.

If the *benefits* of performing a specific exercise outweigh the *costs* (figure 4.2), consider the exercise low risk and unlikely to harm the performer. Table 4.6 demonstrates how risk assessment can be carried out for specific exercises. The "hurdles" stretch has been rated high in terms of benefits because it effectively stretches the hamstring muscle by taking one end of the muscle away from the other. This exercise is also rated high in terms of costs because it places stress on the knee joint and the lower spine. The table recommends that to minimise risk of injury, you should substitute the hurdles stretch for a safer exercise which stretches the hamstrings (see table 2.5, p. 20).

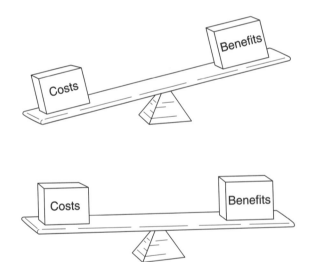

Figure 4.1 The costs outweigh or equal the benefits; the exercise is high risk and is not safe to perform.

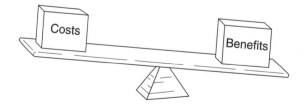

Figure 4.2 The benefits outweigh the costs; the exercise is low risk and is most likely safe to perform.

Table 4.6	Risk Assessment of Specific Exercises			
Cost–benefit analysis	Factors for consideration in risk assessment	Hurdles stretch	Windmills	Sprinting at the start of a warm-up
Benefits	What is the purpose of the exercise or activity?	To stretch the hamstrings.	To mobilise spine or stretch hamstrings or get warm.	To get warm and raise pulse.
	Does it fulfil its purpose?	Yes	Yes	Yes; but participants can easily get too hot working at this intensity.
	Total benefits	High	High	Medium
Costs	*Alignment* Does the exercise move or place joints in ana-tomically correct ways?	No; incorrect alignment of the knee and lower back, stress on medial ligaments and tendons.	No; incorrect alignment of knees, which are locked out to assist balance, incorrect alignment of lumbar spine (hyperflexion and rotation). The lumbar region of the spine does not rotate.	Yes
	Impact Have the risks associated with high-impact activities been minimised?	Yes	Yes	Sprinting cannot be performed for long periods of time.
	Momentum Can the exercise be performed with control?	Yes	Yes	No; sprinting cannot be performed with control; there is not a problem with this activity unless the muscles are cold and less pliable (e.g., at the start of a warm-up).
	Is the exercise appro-priate for children or young people in terms of issues associated with their growth and development?	No; laxity or pain in the knee joint might result from long-term use of this exercise.	No; young people may have long levers and weak muscles, which further increase long-term risk of injury to the spine.	No; young people may have weak or tight muscles which are even more prone to muscle tears if contracted or stretched at speed while still cold.
	Total cost or risk	High	Very high	High
Recommendations for minimising risk		Perform ham-string stretch in a seated position with other knee bent and foot flat on floor.	Mobilise lumbar spine by performing side bends or hip circles.	Raise the pulse gradually; use jogging, skipping or brisk walking.

Sprinting at the start of a warm-up is given a medium to low benefit rating. This activity *does* raise the body temperature and pulse rate, but not in a gradual manner. Participants would find it uncomfortable to go straight into such vigorous activity. They would probably need a rest afterwards, rather than feel ready for action. The costs of this activity are rated high. Sprinting requires major muscles to contract and lengthen at speed and participants may be injured if they sprint with cold, less pliable muscles. In addition, adolescents in a growth spurt may have thin, weak and tight muscles that are less resilient and more susceptible to injury. To minimise the risk of injury, substitute less intense activities that allow participants to control movements and raise their pulse gradually and comfortably (e.g., brisk walking, slow jogging, knee raises).

Including All Pupils

Children and young people with special conditions can participate in exercise, as long as you recognise and understand the symptoms and give appropriate treatment.

Asthma

Asthma is a common respiratory disorder that affects 15 to 25 percent of the school-age population in Britain. Children and young people with asthma are susceptible to their airways narrowing, making breathing difficult. A number of factors can trigger asthma attacks (e.g., irritants, weather changes, viral infections, emotions and exercise). You should recognise and understand the symptoms of asthma and know which young people in your care have asthma. You should also be able to give appropriate treatment.

To help participants with asthma **prepare for activity,** you should

- ensure participants have access to their inhalers; and encourage them to use them before the warm-up;
- forewarn individuals of activities they might need to take particular precautions for (e.g., running outside on a dry, cold day);
- allow individuals to wear a scarf around their mouth and nose in cold or dry weather;
- ensure that the warm-up is very gradual; and
- advise the individual not to take part if they have a cold or viral infection.

To help participants with asthma **recover from activity,** you should

- ensure that the participants have access to their inhalers; exercise-induced asthma is likely to occur during recovery from exercise (usually about 10 minutes after exercise); and
- ensure that there is an effective and gradual cool-down.

Diabetes

Diabetes is caused by a severe failure in the production of the hormone insulin. A child or young person with diabetes either does not produce sufficient insulin or is unable to mobilise the insulin. Insulin acts on glucose in the bloodstream, breaking it down into glycogen to facilitate its removal for energy production and storage in the liver and the muscles. When there is insufficient insulin, excess glucose accumulates in the blood, disrupts the energy production process and the body has to use fat and protein as an energy source. If untreated, this may result in increased acidity of the blood, which can lead to a coma.

You should recognise and understand the symptoms of hypo- and hyperglycaemia, know which young people in your care have diabetes, and be able to give appropriate treatment.

To help participants with diabetes **prepare for activity,** you should

- check before the activity that the participants with diabetes have either eaten a high carbohydrate snack or meal or have altered their insulin injections;
- give individuals advance information concerning the extent and intensity of activities in which they will be involved; and
- ensure that there is some quick-acting, concentrated carbohydrate (e.g., glucose tablet) readily available incase an individual shows signs of hypoglycaemia.

To help participants with diabetes **recover from activity,** ensure that there is some quick-acting, concentrated carbohydrate (e.g., glucose tablet) readily available if an individual suffers from hypoglycaemia.

Excess Body Weight or Obesity

Being overweight means having an excess of body weight relative to height, and obesity is a surplus of fat. This is usually the result of an energy imbalance (i.e., energy intake in terms of food and drink regularly exceeds energy expenditure in terms of exercise or activity). Children and young people who are overweight are likely to have high blood pressure, raised blood sugar levels, reduced ability to perform everyday tasks and social and psychological problems such as low self-esteem.

To help participants who are overweight **prepare for activity,** you should

- let individuals who are overweight wear clothing which is safe, appropriate and in which they feel comfortable and confident;
- ensure that individuals are wearing supportive footwear with a well-cushioned sole;
- ensure that joints are worked in correct alignment and that impact is minimised through safe and effective technique;
- ensure that the warm-up is comfortable and very gradual;
- adapt tasks if necessary (e.g., instead of continuous jogging, alternate 15 seconds of jogging with 15 seconds of brisk walking); and
- constantly monitor individuals, ensure that they feel part of the session and praise and encourage them as appropriate.

To help participants who are overweight **recover from activity,** ensure that the cool-down is effective and gradual. Table 4.7 provides advice on both warming up and cooling down.

Table 4.7 Warming Up and Cooling Down Advice for Teachers

Do	Don't
Involve all participants in activity at the same time.	Have any participants inactive or waiting around for their turn.
Perform exercises with control.	Permit flinging or uncontrolled actions.
Progress gradually (go up steadily through the "gears").	Rush too quickly into fast, rapid activities (e.g., sprinting, jumping, relay races, vigorous tag games).
Ensure that muscles are warm before they are stretched.	Stretch cold muscles.
Hold stretches still.	Bounce while stretching.
Exercise at a comfortable pace.	Exercise so hard that you have to stop.
Exercise at your own pace.	Try to compete or keep up with others.
Try to maintain a tall, straight back when appropriate (e.g., knee lifts, marching).	Put pressure on the lower back by performing exercises with an arched back.
When bending your knees, ensure that they are in line with the ankles and that they are always at least a 90° angle.	Perform deep knee bends or exercises with incorrect alignment of knees (e.g., knees twisting inwards or outwards).
Perform neck mobility exercises with care to avoid trapping nerves or damaging small vertebrae at the top of the spine.	Perform exercises in which the head is forced forwards or backwards or jerked.
Where possible, mix impacts, use safe technique and wear protective footwear.	Perform continuous, high-impact activities with poor technique and with no footwear (e.g., skipping in bare feet).

part II

Practical Ideas

chapter 5

Key Stages 1 and 2 (Ages 5 to 11)

The following ideas are appropriate for use with children at Key Stages 1 and 2. The activities initially require close direction and guidance, particularly in terms of showing and reminding participants how to perform the activities. Once familiar with the activities, some groups will be able to perform them in a more independent manner. This will enable you to observe, assess, correct and give guidance, encouragement and praise.

PRIMARY COLOURS WARM-UP AND COOL-DOWN

Suitable for Key Stage 1 (ages 5 to 7).

Area

Any indoor or outdoor area which is large enough to allow participants to move freely from one place to another.

Equipment

- Four large activity cards
- Beanbags or small balls (sufficient for one between two)

Warm-Up

1. Place the activity cards around the room (see figure 5.1) on walls or prop them on chairs.
2. Help the participants to complete one circuit, performing the two activities on the front of each activity card (e.g., using lead-and-follow). The activities are as follows:
   - **Pass the parcel.** The children stand back to back with a partner and pass a beanbag or small ball 10 times by twisting at the waist to one side and then to the other.
   - **Clap.** The children perform 10 claps. Ask children to clap above their heads, to the side of their body, in front of them or behind their backs. Encourage a variety of claps.
   - **Marching.** The children march 10 times on the spot or travelling, lifting their knees high and using their arms. Discourage children from stamping.
   - **Yes and no!** The children nod or shake their heads, using large controlled actions in response to five simple questions (e.g., Are you breathing faster? Can you feel your heart working?).
   - **Swim to red.** The children walk to the red card and perform any swimming-type movements with their arms (e.g., breaststroke, butterfly, front crawl or backstroke).
   - **Skip to blue.** The children skip (without a rope) to the blue card.
   - **Giant steps to green.** The children travel to the green card, using very large strides that require them to lift their knees high.
3. When children have completed the tasks on the front of all the cards, turn the cards over. Lead the participants through the whole-body stretches on the back of each card (e.g., stretching tall or wide). Hold each stretch still for a slow count of six.

Notes

1. You will need to lead the whole group through the warm-up several times before allowing more confident groups to proceed with less direction.
2. As the participants become familiar with the activities in the circuit and are able to associate the words with the actions, allow some individuals to try the warm-up independently. You could divide participants who are very familiar with this warm-up into four groups, each group starting at a different colour.
3. The children can perform the circuit to 20 to 30 seconds of music followed by a gap (during which the participants switch to the next activity).
4. Paint the colours onto the activity cards or make the cards of the appropriate colour.

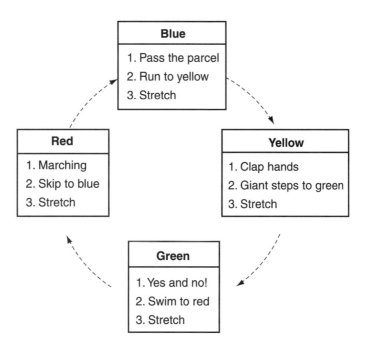

Figure 5.1 The four activity cards needed for the Primary Colours Warm-Up and Cool-Down drill.

Cool-Down

The participants can repeat some of the actions on the activity cards, such as the travelling moves and the stretches. Encourage them to hold each stretch still for a slow count of 10.

CIRCLES AND SHAPES WARM-UP AND COOL-DOWN

Suitable for Key Stage 1 (ages 5 to 7).

Area

Any indoor area.

Equipment

- Music machine and music (optional)

Warm-Up

1. Instruct the participants to travel anywhere in the space, using stepping actions. Use prompts to encourage variety, for example, "Can you use little steps, big steps, are you going forwards, backwards or sideways?"
2. Call out "Circles". The participants stop travelling and draw large circles with a variety of body parts, for example, hands, elbows, feet, knees, head or hips. Children should perform these actions with control. Use prompts to encourage variety (e.g., "Show me how you can draw large circles with your elbows, show me how you can draw large circles with your toes"). Ask the participants to resume travelling again.
3. Call out "Shapes". The participants stop travelling and change between wide, straight, curled and twisted body shapes. These actions should be continuous and controlled. Use prompts to encourage variety, for example, "Show me a wide shape that is close to the floor, make a curled shape while you are standing up".
4. Repeat activities one to three in any order until the participants are warm.
5. Lead the participants through some whole-body stretches (e.g., stretch tall, stretch wide). The participants should hold each stretch still for a slow count of six.

Notes

1. Use three different pieces of music or three different musical instruments (e.g., suspended cymbal, tambourine, wood block) to indicate the three different activities (travelling, circles and shapes). The participants change activity in response to a change in the music or instrument used.
2. Children can perform the shapes and circles on mats and can "travel" around the mats.

Cool-Down

Ask participants to repeat warm-up activities two and three, gradually decreasing the speed of the movements and then to perform activity five. The participants should hold each stretch still for a slow count of 10.

WARM-UP AND COOL-DOWN WITH A BALL

Suitable for Key Stage 1 (ages 5 to 7).

Area

Any large indoor area or outdoor area.

Equipment

- Large balls (one per pair)   • Marker cones, grids or playground lines

Warm-Up

1. Organise the participants and the equipment as indicated in figure 5.2.
2. **A** carries the ball in his or her hands and skips towards and around **B** and back to his or her place. **A** rolls the ball towards **B**, who receives it using his or her hands. **B** then skips around **A**, carrying the ball, and rolls the ball to **A**. Repeat this activity several times.
3. Partners stand back to back and pass the ball over their heads and under their legs. Participants should perform this using their shoulders to pass the ball overhead and bending their knees to pass the ball under their legs. Repeat this activity several times. Partners should change direction in order to experience receiving as well as passing the ball overhead.
4. **A** carries the ball in his or her hands and skips towards and around **B** and back to his or her place. **A** then throws the ball towards **B**, who receives it using his or her hands (the ball can bounce several times before it is received). **B** then skips around **A**, carrying the ball, and throws it to **A**. Repeat this activity several times.
5. Partners stand back to back and twist their upper body to pass the ball to each other. Remind participants to perform this carefully and to change direction after several repeats to avoid becoming dizzy!
6. When the participants are warm, lead them through one or two whole-body stretches (e.g., stretch tall, stretch wide). They should hold each stretch still for a slow count of six.

Cool-Down

Ask children to perform activities two or four, after which hold one or two whole-body stretches still for a slow count of 10.

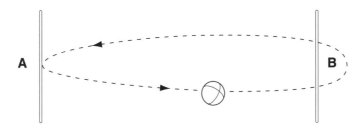

Figure 5.2 The positioning of the participants and equipment for the Warm-Up and Cool-Down With a Ball drill.

GENERAL WARM-UP AND COOL-DOWN

Suitable for Key Stages 1 and 2 (ages 5 to 11).

Area

Any indoor or outdoor area.

Equipment

- Board or card (optional)
- Marker pens (optional)

Warm-Up

Lead the participants through the activities shown in table 5.1.

Notes

1. This warm-up is suitable for many activities and could be written on a large card and placed in a hall or gym for participants to follow independently at the beginning of lessons, at the start of lunchtime or after school activities.
2. You may need to amend the terminology used to suit the participants.
3. You may need to help participants read and interpret the guidelines.
4. Extend the repertoire of exercises as participants' movement vocabulary increases. For example, use additional pulse-raising activities, such as skipping, sidestepping and galloping, in addition to jogging and marching. Older participants can start to incorporate stretches for specific muscle groups (e.g., calves, hamstrings) instead of whole-body stretches.

Cool-Down

Lead the participants through the activities in table 5.2.

Table 5.1	General Warm-Up for Key Stages 1 and 2 (Ages 5 to 11)
1	3 laps (skipping).
2	6 small knee lifts on the spot.
3	3 large shoulder circles backwards.
4	3 large shoulder circles forwards.
	Stand still, hands on waist, and do
	• 6 head tilts (head towards shoulder),
	• 6 side bends, and
	• 6 body twists (look over your shoulder but keep the bottom half of your body facing forwards).
5	3 laps (skipping).
6	20 marches on the spot–high knees, use arms.
7	2 whole-body stretches (e.g., stretch tall, stretch wide); hold each for a slow count of 6.
8	Shake out arms and legs.

Table 5.2	General Cool-Down for Key Stages 1 and 2 (Ages 5 to 11)
1	Skip 1 lap.
2	Brisk walk 1 lap.
3	Do 2 whole-body stretches (e.g., long and tall, wide); hold each for a slow count of 10.
4	Shake out arms and legs.

TRAFFIC WARM-UP AND COOL-DOWN

Suitable for Key Stages 1 and 2 (ages 5 to 11).

Area

Any indoor or outdoor area which allows the participants to move freely around a circuit marked out with cones. The circuit can be large if the space allows.

Equipment

- Traffic-light cards (red, amber, green—at least two of each) • Cones (same number as traffic-lights cards) • Six extra cones to make a roundabout in the centre of the working space

Warm-Up

1. Attach the traffic-light cards to the cones and position them in a clear circuit formation in the playing area.
2. Lead the whole group around one circuit and demonstrate how the participants should respond to each traffic-light card. For example, at the red traffic-light cone, participants should stop and perform the mobilising exercises described before travelling onto the next cone (see table 5.3).
3. At any time during the circuit call out "Roundabout". When this happens all participants leave the circuit and jog or skip around the central roundabout before returning to the circuit. Indicate the direction in which participants should travel around the roundabout.
4. When the group is warm, instruct them to stop at the next red traffic light.
5. Participants perform some whole-body stretches (e.g., stretch tall, stretch wide). Ask them to hold each stretch still for a slow count of six.

Notes

1. Allow individuals who are very familiar with the circuit to travel around it independently.
2. Older participants might like to be involved in setting up the circuit and deciding the route that the "vehicles" will take. They might decide to incorporate other Highway Code signs and features (e.g., speed limit signs to indicate the intensity at which the participants jog, or contraflow signs to involve the participants jogging in zigzag pathways to change traffic lanes).
3. Instead of using cards, you can call out the colours of the traffic lights as the participants travel around a coned circuit. Give children time to respond appropriately before calling out the next colour.

Cool-Down

The cool-down does not require traffic-light cards, but the coned circuit remains. Call out "Green" and "Roundabout" more frequently in the initial stages of the cool-down to ensure that the participants keep moving. Reduce the exercise intensity gradually by calling out "Amber" more frequently and, in the latter stages, by calling out a mixture of "Amber" and "Red" before the participants perform their cool-down stretches. Participants should hold each stretch still for a slow count of 10.

Table 5.3	Activities for Traffic Warm-Up
Green	Jog gently to the next traffic sign.
Amber	Walk briskly to the next traffic sign.
Red	Stop and stand tall; do 6 shoulder circles, 6 upper-body twists and 6 side bends.

RUNAWAY TRAINS WARM-UP AND COOL-DOWN

Suitable for Key Stages 1 and 2 (ages 5 to 11).

Area

Any indoor or outdoor area which allows participants to travel at different speeds.

Equipment

- Six or more cones, skittles or markers

Warm-Up

1. Participants form one long line behind you. Tell them that you are the engine and they are the carriages of a train that is about to go on a journey. They must keep one behind the other and close together during the journey (see figure 5.3).

2. The train takes a winding route around the cones that are spaced out in the area. Maintain verbal and visual contact with participants at the back of the line. Begin by walking slowly and then alternate between brisk walking, skipping and slow jogging.

3. While the train is travelling, the participants can mobilise their shoulders and elbows by performing piston-type movements with their arms. They can make these movements larger as the train goes "uphill" or is "pulling a heavy load", and smaller as it travels on the flat ground.

4. The train can stop from time to time at a station (e.g., beside a cone). Whilst at the station lead the participants through the following activities to mobilise joints:

   - "Passengers coming aboard!" (Participants lift their knees high.)

   - "Loading heavy luggage!" (Participants put their hands on their hips and face forwards; they bend to one side and then the other to simulate heavy luggage being loaded onto each side of the train.)

   - "Ready to go?" (Participants look back along the platform to see if the guard is about to signal for the train to leave the station. By holding the waist of the "carriage" in front, the children twist the top half of their body to look behind them one way and then the other.)

5. When the participants are warm and all the joints have been mobilised the train stops at another station to stretch the muscles. This can include general body stretches (such as stretching tall, stretching wide) or more specific stretches for the legs (e.g., calf stretch) and upper body (e.g., chest stretch), depending on the level of knowledge and understanding of the participants. They should hold each stretch still for a slow count of six.

6. The train continues on its journey, but this time it occasionally becomes a "runaway train", which involves short bursts of high-speed work. Lead the group and try to follow high-speed work with an "uphill" walk, before increasing the speed again. This should enable the whole group to stay together and to recover between energetic bursts of speed.

Figure 5.3   The line-up of participants for the Runaway Trains Warm-Up and Cool-Down drill.

Notes

1. When they are familiar with the idea, the group can split into two or more trains. The trains should not collide and should keep out of each other's way. A coned circuit might help with the organisation of this activity.

2. Direct the trains verbally and tell them what they are doing next, for example, "The train is going up a big hill and the pistons are working very hard."

3. Ask another person in the line to take on the role of the engine, for example, "The third person in the line is now the engine—follow them!" The appointed person comes to the front of the train.

Cool-Down

The train travels quite quickly at the beginning of the cool-down and gradually slows down (e.g., by going up imaginary hills or by running out of fuel). The train can then stop to stretch out the muscles. These can include general body stretches (e.g., stretch tall, stretch wide) or more specific stretches for the legs (e.g., calf stretch) and upper body (e.g., chest stretch), depending on the level of knowledge and understanding of the participants. The participants should hold each stretch still for a slow count of 10.

chapter 6

Key Stages 2 and 3 (Ages 7 to 14)

The following warm-ups and cool-downs are appropriate for use with children at Key Stages 2 and 3 (ages 7 to 14). The activities initially require direction and guidance, but with practice, participants should be able to perform them in a more independent manner. This will enable you to observe, assess, correct and give guidance, encouragement and praise.

GENERAL WARM-UP

Suitable for Key Stages 2 and 3 (ages 7 to 14).

Area

Any indoor or outdoor area.

Equipment

- Board or card (optional)   • Marker pens (optional)   • Worksheets (optional)

Warm-Up

Participants follow the guidelines in table 6.1. You can write the guidelines on a board, large card or on worksheets, or you can make photocopies of table 6.1 for participants as needed. Participants work individually or in twos or threes.

Table 6.1	General Warm-Up for Key Stages 2 and 3 (Ages 7 to 14)
1	3 laps: jogging, sidestepping and crossing feet over. Increase your pulse rate gradually.
2	On the spot, perform • 6 side bends, • 6 upper-body twists, and • 6 head tilts.
3	Travel anywhere–jogging, skipping (without a rope) and sidestepping. Do shoulder shrugs, shoulder circles or arm circles while you are travelling.
4	On the spot, perform • 6 hip circles, • 6 knee lifts, and • 6 marches.
5	Stretch the muscles in the • back of the lower leg, and • back of the upper leg. Hold each still for a slow count of 6.
6	Jog on the spot for a count of 10. Run fast on the spot for a count of 10. Repeat this 6 times. Pump your arms while you are running fast.
7	Stretch the muscles in the • front of the upper leg, and • inside of the upper leg. Hold each still for a slow count of 6.
8	March or jog on the spot and stretch the muscles in the • chest, • upper back, and • back of the upper arm. Hold each still for a slow count of 6.
9	Shake out your arms and legs.

Figure 6.1 Stretch for the muscles in the back of the upper leg (hamstrings).

Figure 6.2 Stretch for the muscles in the chest (pectorals).

Notes

1. This warm-up is suitable for many activities. You could write it on a large card and place it in a hall or gym for more experienced participants to follow independently at the beginning of lessons, at the start of lunchtime or after school activities.

2. You may have to amend the terminology used to suit the needs of the participants.

3. This warm-up assumes that participants are aware of the purpose of mobility, pulse-raising or -lowering and stretching exercises, and have learnt how to perform these safely and effectively (e.g., with controlled movements in the mobility and pulse-raising or -lowering exercises and with static stretches).

4. You can assess the participants' knowledge and understanding of warming up and cooling down whilst they are completing the tasks.

Cool-Down

Participants follow the guidelines from table 6.2. You can write the guidelines on a board, large card or on worksheets, or you can make photocopies of table 6.2 for participants as needed. Participants can work individually or in twos or threes.

Table 6.2	General Cool-Down for Key Stages 2 and 3 (Ages 7 to 14)
1	1 lap–brisk walk.
2	Stretch the muscles in the • chest, • upper back, and • back of upper arm. Hold each still for a slow count of 10.
3	Travel 2 laps–jogging, sidestepping and brisk walking. Bring your pulse rate down gradually.
4	Stretch the muscles in the • back of the lower leg, and • back of the upper leg.
5	Shake out the arms and legs.

Figure 6.3 Stretch for the muscles in the back of the upper leg (hamstrings).

Figure 6.4 Stretch for the muscles on the inside of the upper leg (adductors or groin).

Suitable for Key Stages 2 and 3 (ages 7 to 14).

Area

Swimming pool.

Equipment

- Floats

Warm-Up

1. Explain that Alcatraz was a maximum-security prison in San Francisco harbour, which was surrounded by water. The only way to escape was to swim across the bay, and this had to be done very quietly in order that the guards on lookout did not notice. Searchlights scoured the water from time to time and the escaping prisoners had to duck quietly under the water for a moment to avoid being spotted.

2. Challenge participants to swim or wade a number of lengths or widths of the pool slowly and carefully and to respond to searchlights by ducking quietly under the water before resurfacing. Hold up a float in each hand to indicate when the searchlights are on.

3. Instruct participants to gradually increase their speed as the escaping prisoners swim further away from the island. Ask the participants to stop at any point and tread water or march on the spot. From this position they can mobilise their shoulders, elbows and wrists by waving for help in various ways, as directed.

4. At the end of the warm-up, the participants reach land and perform stretches in the water or after lifting themselves out of the water. They should hold each stretch still for 6 to 10 seconds.

Notes

If all participants can swim in deep water, ask them to perform the activity along the length of the pool. If not, they can use the width of the pool. This enables them to work in a depth of water that is comfortable for them.

If the swimming session to follow is unlikely to take the group's muscles to the end of their range of movement at speed, it may not be necessary to perform warm-up stretches. Intersperse the stretches with lively, pulse-raising activities as this will help to keep the body warm.

Cool-Down

Challenge participants to complete a number of lengths or widths of the pool as calmly and quietly as possible. The same 'searchlight' rules apply as for the warm-up. The participants perform whole-body stretches in the water or as soon as they have lifted themselves out of the water. Ask them to hold each stretch still for 10 to 20 seconds.

INVASION GAMES WARM-UP AND COOL-DOWN

Suitable for Key Stages 2 and 3 (ages 7 to 13).

Area

Any large indoor or outdoor area which allows participants to travel at different speeds.

Equipment

- None

Warm-Up

1. Participants walk or jog at a brisk pace to all four corners of the area. They travel back through the centre after visiting each corner.

2. Participants stop and mobilise the hip and knee joints, using exercises such as hip circles and knee lifts. They should perform these in a smooth, controlled manner.

3. Participants jog to the corners again and, at the same time, mobilise the shoulders, using exercises such as shoulder lifts and arm circles (backwards and forwards).

4. Participants stop and mobilise the spine, using exercises such as side bends and upper-body twists. They should perform these in a smooth, controlled manner.

5. Participants jog up to any line marked on the floor or ground, and pivot away from it. They can pivot off either foot. Participants can pivot away from each other if lines are not available. Encourage them to look up and be aware of the space and of each other.

6. Participants stretch the muscles on the inside of the upper leg (groin or adductors) and the back of the upper leg (hamstrings). They should hold each stretch still for 6 to 10 seconds.

7. Participants jog forwards and, now and again, perform small, dodging actions to the left (i.e., pushing off the right foot and taking the body across to the left). They can perform this in pairs, with participants running towards and dodging around each other (i.e., both dodging to their own left). Repeat the activity, dodging to the right.

Figure 6.5 Partner stretch for the muscles in the back of the lower leg (gastrocnemius).

Figure 6.6 Partner stretch for the muscles in the front of the upper leg (quadriceps).

Figure 6.7 Performing a two-footed jump with a partner, clapping hands raised above the head (high-fives jump).

8. Participants stretch the muscles in the back of the lower leg (calf) and front of the upper leg (quadriceps). Ask them to hold each stretch still for 6 to 10 seconds. Participants can use each other for support (see figures 6.5 and 6.6).

9. Participants perform a two-footed jump and raise hands into the air (as if catching a ball). They can synchronise this activity with a partner (jogging towards each other and both jumping up and clapping hands above head height, see figure 6.7).

10. Participants accelerate into open spaces and slow down to a jogging pace on arrival.

Notes

1. Once the group has stretched, develop some of the more energetic ideas. Develop jumping and clapping as a challenge in which participants count the number of times they can perform this activity with different people in 20 seconds.

2. Incorporate games skills, such as footwork, dodging, marking and spacing, into the warm-up to help to provide an early focus to the session and to use movements relevant to later activities.

3. If the invasion game involves upper-body movements, such as throwing and catching, include stretches for the muscles in the chest (pectorals), the back of the upper arm (triceps) and the upper back (trapezius and rhomboids).

4. Towards the end of the warm-up ask participants to run around and, when you call out a number, to get themselves into the appropriate group sizes (e.g., threes, sixes, eights, ones, fours, finishing with the number required for the next activity).

Cool-Down

• Encourage participants to keep their legs moving (e.g., by jogging, side-stepping or brisk walking). This can be achieved by travelling back to the changing rooms. Ask participants to stretch the muscles in the chest (pectorals) and the back of the upper arm (triceps) whilst travelling. They should hold each stretch still for 10 to 20 seconds.

• Where possible, make sure the group performs stretches for the muscles in the back of the upper leg (hamstrings), front of the upper leg (quadriceps), back of the lower leg (calf) and inside of the upper leg (groin or adductors), in relaxed and comfortable positions (e.g., seated or lying down). Ask participants to hold each stretch still for 10 to 20 seconds. The group can perform these stretches outside or in the changing rooms. If performed outside on a cold day, intersperse the stretching with jogging or marching to keep the muscles warm. Encourage the use of benches, walls and trees for variety or additional support during stretches.

DANCE WARM-UP AND COOL-DOWN

Suitable for Key Stages 2 and 3 (ages 7 to 14).

Area

An indoor area that allows participants to move amongst each other freely while travelling.

Equipment

- Music machine and music (optional)

Warm-Up

1. Posture check: participants take the body off centre by gently swaying forwards and backwards and side to side and then finding a place in which the weight is distributed evenly on both feet. Help the participants to check that their
   - hips are placed over the knees,
   - knees are not locked out,
   - shoulders are relaxed and over the hips,
   - tummy muscles are pulled tight and spine is in natural alignment.

   For the purposes of this warm-up, this is called centring.
2. Participants walk anywhere in the space and pause to centre the body when asked.
3. The group changes direction while walking and pauses to centre when asked.
4. Participants travel swiftly in the space and make three changes of direction before centering. Repeat this sequence two or three times.
5. Lead the group through the following mobility motifs. The groups should perform both motifs with continuous and controlled actions:

   Motif one to mobilise the shoulders, the thoracic area of the spine and the neck:
   - Take one straight arm forwards, upwards and backwards in a full circle and finish with the arm reaching to the ceiling ("backstroke and reach").
   - Draw a line with the same lifted hand as it descends along the mid-line of the body.
   - Follow the hand with the eyes and roll down through the spine gently, keeping the chin as close to the body as possible and the top of the head facing the toes. The knees should be bent and in line with the ankles (i.e., not knocking inwards), and the bottom tucked under.
   - Uncurl the spine, making sure that the shoulders and head are the last parts of the spine to uncurl. The abdominal muscles should assist this movement. The hands can be left by the sides.
   - Twist gently to the right and left, making sure that the hips stay facing forwards and that the body is upright. Extend the arms to the sides as the body returns to the centre after each twist. Allow the body to follow the arms after two or three twists to each side (the resulting action will be an off-balance turn), after which the participants can travel as in 5 earlier, before stopping to repeat the mobilising phase, using the other arm or using both arms.

   Motif two to mobilise the lumbar region of the spine, the neck, the hips and the ankles:
   - From a centred position, turn the head to look over one shoulder and then the other and then look forwards again (look to the side, centre, side, centre).
   - Bend to the side as if picking up a bag, making sure that the body does not tilt and the hips are kept centred. Repeat this to the other side after pausing momentarily in the centre.

- Circle the hips, keeping your hands on your hips.
- Lift both arms upwards, as if taking a jumper off over the head, and complete this action by reaching up with both arms over the head. Lean forwards and let the heels lift as this action is performed.
- Balance, tilt and tip and then travel, changing direction three times before stopping and centring.

6. Ask participants to perform motifs one and two several times and to travel (changing direction three times) before stopping and centering the body in preparation to perform either motif.

7. Ask participants to develop the motifs by performing the movements in any order and to mix and match parts of the motifs. They can alternate these with travelling and pausing to centre the body.

8. Choreograph the stretches into a third motif. The stretches you include are determined by the movements to be included in the dance session. Ask participants to hold each stretch still for 6 to 10 seconds.

Notes

1. A dance warm-up should allow participants to become accustomed to the working space and to the other people in the group. It should assist psychological preparation and allow familiarity with the mood and flow of the movements included in the main part of the session.

2. A development of the warm-up motifs can involve participants designing duets in which the mobility motifs are performed by both dancers in a question or answer mode in unison or in cannon. Ask participants to refine their work and to evaluate their own or others' work using prompt sheets.

Cool-Down

Ask the participants to perform motif one using both arms in the reaching action and breathing in as they do this. They release an outward breath as the arms descend down the mid-line of the body. Alternate this motif with travelling actions that are swift at the beginning of the cool-down and gradually decrease in intensity as the cool-down progresses. Each time the group repeats motif one, the movements become slightly less energetic, for example, the circling and reaching movement is executed by both arms during the first performance and subsequently by one arm only, the elbows, and finally, just the shoulders. Participants should hold the cool-down stretches still for 10 to 20 seconds in comfortable, relaxed positions; the transitions should be smooth and calm.

SWIMMING WARM-UP AND COOL-DOWN

Suitable for Key Stages 2 and 3 (ages 7 to 14).

Area

Swimming pool (the group can perform the activities in deep or shallow water depending on the group's range of ability).

Equipment

- Floats

Warm-Up

1. Ask participants to start in a space and travel anywhere in the pool at a comfortable pace whilst maintaining the same distance from the other participants (restrict the space if teaching a small group in a large pool). Participants need to be able to observe those around them and, for safety, should perform strokes using a "head up" action.

2. Ask participants to stop traveling and tread water or march on the spot while you give the next instruction.

3. Ask participants to accelerate into any space that is created in the pool. Once they have accelerated into the new space, they can slow down again until another space appears.

4. Ask participants to stop moving, to find a partner and to come to the side of the pool for the next instruction.

5. Working in pairs, the participants tread water or march while facing a partner. One partner leads the other through some mobility exercises for the shoulders, elbows and wrists. They should perform these movements in a smooth and controlled manner. Change the leader and repeat the activity.

6. Working in pairs, the participants tread water or march while facing each other. The participants push down very hard with their hands and feet to lift the shoulders and upper body clear of the water (as in the preparation for a feet-first surface dive). Individuals attempt to synchronise this pushing action in order to clap their partner's hands as they reach the highest point above the water. Non-swimmers can perform a jumping action in shallow water to achieve the same effect.

7. Ask the group to perform stretches in the following ways. They should hold each stretch still for 6 to 10 seconds. Encourage participants to swim, wade or perform astride jumps between stretches to ensure that their muscles stay warm.

Notes

If the swimming session to follow is unlikely to take the group's muscles to the end of their range of movement at speed, it may not be necessary to perform warm-up stretches. Intersperse the stretches with lively, pulse-raising activities as this will help to keep the body warm.

Cool-Down

Participants perform activities 5 and 6 and then perform activities 1 and 3. Make sure the group performs cool-down stretches on dry land if this is a warmer environment.

MUSICAL SWIMMING WARM-UP AND COOL-DOWN

Suitable for Key Stages 2 and 3 (ages 7 to 14).

Area

Swimming pool (the temperature needs to be quite warm).

Equipment

- Music machine   • Music (three pieces lasting for 60 to 90 seconds each)   • Floats

Warm-Up

1. Ask participants to swim, wade or move about in the water in a way that reflects the mood of the music being played. You might need to specify an appropriate direction of travel (e.g., along the length, across the width). With some groups, you could allow a completely free choice of direction of travel.

2. For the warm-up, the mood of the music needs to start in a calm manner and gradually become livelier to encourage more energetic actions.

3. Stretch the muscles that will be used in the main activity. Ask participants to hold stretches still for 6 to 10 seconds. Intersperse the stretches with some lively, pulse-raising activities (e.g., jogging, jumping and twisting) to keep the muscles warm.

Notes

If the swimming session to follow is unlikely to take muscles to the end of their range of movement at speed, participants may not need to perform warm-up stretches.

Cool-Down

For the cool-down, the mood of each piece of music needs to be progressively calmer. The final piece of music should be very calm and peaceful and participants might like to use floats to help them relax. They can perform gentle movements of their limbs whilst floating. If the pool temperature is warm, the group can stretch in the water.

JOG AND RUN WARM-UP AND COOL-DOWN

Suitable for Key Stages 2 and 3 (ages 7 to 14).

Area

Any indoor or outdoor area.

Equipment

- None

Warm-Up

1. Participants walk briskly or jog gently for at least three to four minutes until they feel warm. This process might take longer in cold conditions. Swinging or gently pumping the arms will mobilise the shoulder and elbow joints.

2. If the warm-up is for running, make sure the group stretches the muscles in the back of the lower leg (calf), the upper leg (hamstrings), the front of the upper leg (quadriceps) and inside of the upper leg (groin or adductors). Ask the group to hold each of these stretches still for 6 to 10 seconds. If stretching outside in cold weather, participants need to jog around or march between stretches to prevent the muscles from becoming cold.

Notes

1. Older participants should be able to warm up independently. You may need to direct younger and less experienced individuals through the warm-up, particularly the stretches.

2. If the participants' knowledge of stretching is limited, the priority stretches for jogging and running are the muscles in the back of the lower leg (calf) and the back of the upper leg (hamstrings). Over time, add stretches for the front of the upper leg (quadriceps), inside of the upper leg (groin or adductors) and muscles from the top of the leg to the pelvis or lower back (hip flexors).

3. Include specific mobility exercises for the spine and hips and pulse-raising activities (e.g., "sprinters' arms" and "high knees") if the activity to follow is intense.

Cool-Down

1. Participants jog gently or walk for a couple of minutes to gradually lower their pulse. They should not stand still or sit down immediately after jogging or running.

2. Participants perform static stretches for the main muscle groups involved. For jogging and running these are the muscles in the back of the lower leg (calf). Make sure participants stretch the muscles in the back of the upper leg (hamstrings) before running. Over time, you can add stretches for the front of the upper leg (quadriceps), inside of the upper leg (groin or adductors) and muscles from the top of the leg to the pelvis or lower back (hip flexors). Ask participants to hold each stretch still for 10 to 20 seconds and perform the stretches, where possible, in comfortable, relaxed positions. If stretching outside in cold weather, encourage the group to jog around or march between stretches to prevent the muscles from becoming cold.

WAFFLE WARM-UP AND COOL-DOWN

Suitable for Key Stages 2 and 3 (ages 7 to 14).

Area

A very large indoor or outdoor area is required.

Equipment

- Activity cones   • "Waffle" cards (optional)

Warm-Up

1. Ask participants to walk briskly or jog in pairs on a specified route and, whilst walking or jogging, to chat or "waffle" about a particular topic (e.g., hobbies, television programmes, health, pets, music, holidays, homework, pocket money, fitness). You can call out the topics or write them on cards and place them around the route (on cones, trees, walls or fences).

2. Develop this idea using activity cones to make four different coloured routes (e.g., red, yellow, blue and white). Participants can help to set out the cones at the start of the lesson. Zigzag, circular, square and straight-line routes can be designed, with all routes starting and finishing at the same point. The routes should be different lengths and set out in different directions. Participants travel along all four routes in any order, returning to the central point after each one.

3. Give participants a topic before they start each route. Call out the topics or write them on cards.

4. Participants can perform mobility exercises whilst jogging (e.g., shoulder shrugs, arm circles) or after completing each route, although this depends on the activity to follow.

5. On the last route and to help with equipment collection, you can ask participants to pick up the activity cones as they travel past. Alternatively, leave the cones in position for use in the cool-down.

6. The group can perform stretches for the main muscles to be used in the following activity at the central point or after completing all four routes. The amount of direction and guidance required will depend on participants' level of knowledge and understanding. Hold each stretch still for 6 to 10 seconds.

Notes

1. A variation of this idea might involve participants collecting the cones on their last warm-up route and setting them out again in a different formation, thus creating new routes which you can use in the warm-up, main activity or cool-down.

2. A development of the "waffle" idea would be to use a particular theme (e.g., healthy lifestyles, healthy exercise, healthy eating) and to use opportunities (e.g., during the stretching) to obtain feedback from the participants on their thoughts and views.

Cool-Down

Participants walk or jog on specified routes (e.g., around the perimeter of the field or along the routes set out by cones) and discuss what they have learnt in the session and use their feedback to help conclude the lesson. Make sure the group stretches the main muscle groups used in the session between routes or after completing the last route. Ask participants to hold each stretch still for 10 to 20 seconds and perform them, where possible, in comfortable, relaxed positions.

THE GEARS WARM-UP AND COOL-DOWN

Suitable for Key Stages 2 and 3 (ages 7 to 14).

Area

Any indoor or outdoor space which allows participants to travel in a circuit around cones, line markings or grids.

Equipment

- Cones or line markings

Warm-Up

1. Before starting, explain to the group that this activity involves gradually increasing exercise intensity by working through the five 'gears' of a car. Individuals need to work out for themselves how the exercise should feel to them in each 'gear.'

2. Participants jog around a circuit marked with cones, lines or natural landmarks (e.g., trees, bushes) and you call out the number of the gear they should be working in (e.g., first gear). The participants adjust their speed according to the gear in which they are travelling.

3. At the start of the warm-up call out only gears 'one' and 'two', and suggest that the arms and shoulders are mobilised while they are travelling.

4. Participants need to change to 'neutral' (stationary) in order to perform mobility exercises for the spine, neck and hips before going up through the gears again. As the warm-up progresses, you can introduce 'third gear'.

5. Participants perform stretches. Ask participants to hold each stretch still for 6 to 10 seconds.

6. After the stretches, call out any of the five gears for a short period of time. This will allow the participants to run at top speed (in gear five) and to use both aerobic and anaerobic energy systems.

Notes

1. When the participants are familiar with the warm-up, you might use additional words such as 'reverse' and 'turbo' to add humour to the activity.

2. You could conduct the same warm-up over a straight course, as follows:
   - The participants pick up a card at one end of the course which indicates the gear that they should use to travel to the other end of the course. Only use gears one to three at this stage in the warm-up.
   - On arrival at the other end of the course, the participants pick up another.
   - If participants select a neutral card, they should remain at the same end of the course and mobilise two joints (e.g., upper spine and lower spine) before selecting another card.
   - When they have completed at least six cards, participants should mobilise any joints not covered in the first part of the warm-up. They should then stretch the muscles to be used in the main activity. They should hold each stretch still for 6 to 10 seconds.
   - When participants have stretched the muscles, they continue to select cards from the piles at either end of the track, but this time remove the neutral cards and add the higher gear cards (e.g., gears four and five).

3. Adapt the warm-up by using the names of different modes of transport instead of gears to indicate the exercise intensity to the participants (e.g., scooter, bicycle, mountain bike, racing bike, motorbike). Ask participants to select their own names of vehicles for this purpose.

Cool-Down

Gradually decrease the exercise intensity by working back down through the gears. Use gears two and three in the centre section of the cool-down and gears one and two in the final section. Participants perform stretches in comfortable and relaxed positions where possible, holding each stretch still for 10 to 20 seconds.

RELAY WARM-UP AND COOL-DOWN

Suitable for Key Stages 2 and 3 (ages 7 to 14).

Area

Any indoor or outdoor area which allows groups to travel in a straight line and perform relay-type activities.

Equipment

- Two beanbags or balls (any size) per relay team

Warm-Up

1. Divide the group into relay teams with eight to ten participants in each team.
2. Half the members of each team are positioned at one end of the space and half at the other (as shown in figure 6.8). Each half of the team has a ball or beanbag.
3. Half of each team form a queue and pass the ball or beanbag along the line by twisting from the waist and passing it to the person behind them, or by passing alternately over their heads and between their legs (with bent knees).
4. At the same time the other half of the team jog steadily from their end of the course around the rest of their team and back to their starting place. While they are jogging, they perform mobility exercises for the shoulders.
5. The two halves of each team swap roles.
6. When activities 3 and 4 have completed activity 5, one half of each team performs short chest passes to each other using the ball. The other half travels down the course and around them, using sideways shuffling and galloping actions. The arms can be brought alternately across the body and out to the sides to continue to mobilise the shoulders. The halves of the team swap roles.
7. When both halves of each team have completed activity 6, call out the name or location of muscle groups to be stretched. All team members jog towards each other from the two ends of the course and, choose a partner in the other half of the team, and perform appropriate stretches (e.g., calf and quadriceps stretches; see figures 6.5 and 6.6). The pair should hold each stretch still for 6 to 10 seconds.
8. Label the two halves of each team "sharks" and "shrimps" and ask them to stand in two lines about a metre apart and opposite their partners. Call out "sharks" or "shrimps". If "sharks" is called, the "sharks" chase and try to tag the "shrimps" as they run back to a starting line. Repeat this activity several times.

Cool-Down

Participants can cool-down by repeating the travelling and stretching activities described in the warm-up. They should hold each cool-down stretch still for 10 to 20 seconds and perform the stretches, where possible, in comfortable, relaxed positions.

Figure 6.8 Positioning of teams for the Relay Warm-Up and Cool-Down drill.

LUCKY SPOT WARM-UP AND COOL-DOWN

Suitable for Key Stages 2 and 3 (ages 7 to 14).

Area

Any indoor or outdoor area that is large enough to allow participants to travel around the perimeter freely.

Equipment

• Music machine and music (optional) • Lucky Spot cards (see table 6.3). The Lucky Spot cards include mobility, pulse-raising or -lowering and stretching exercises on separate cards. Make a note of the numbers of the cards which refer to particular elements of the warm-up and cool-down (e.g., cards 2, 4, 9, 11 and 13 are mobility exercises).

Warm-Up

1. Place the Lucky Spot cards with the number side uppermost on the floor around the perimeter of the area.

2. The participants jog around the room. After a short while ask them to stop. Call out a lucky number. The participant who is positioned nearest to this card, or who has picked it up, leads the rest of the group in the activity described on the reverse of the card. You may need to assist less confident individuals.

3. At first, you should call out only the numbers of the cards relating to mobility and pulse-raising exercises. Participants perform the activity on each Lucky Spot card until you (or the music) indicate that they should jog around the room again. As soon as the participants are sufficiently warm, include the stretching cards. Participants should hold each stretch still for 6 to 10 seconds.

Notes

1. Use music to determine when the participants jog around the perimeter. When the music stops, participants stop next to or pick up a card.

Table 6.3	Lucky Spot Warm-Up
Card number	**Activity**
1	March on the spot (knees high)
2	Arm circles
3	Sidestepping into the centre and back
4	Hip circles
5	Calf stretch (back of lower leg)
6	Knee lifts
7	Astride jumps
8	Fast walking (around the outside of the circle)
9	Skipping into the centre and back
10	Upper-body twists
11	Hamstring stretch (back of upper leg)
12	Race walking (around the outside of the circle)
13	Jogging (around the outside of the circle)
14	Quadriceps stretch (front of upper leg)
15	Head tilts (head towards shoulder)
16	Knee bends

2. The Lucky Spot cards can be very specific concerning the exercises participants need to complete (e.g., eight knee lifts with alternate legs on the spot, brisk walk). As participants become more knowledgeable about warming up and cooling down, you can make the cards less specific (e.g., mobilise your knees and hips, raise your pulse gradually). This acts as a potential assessment tool.

Cool-Down

Call out card numbers representing the less energetic travelling activities. After this, call out the card numbers representing stretches. The group should hold each stretch still for 10 to 20 seconds and perform the stretches, where possible, in comfortable, relaxed positions.

CHANGE-THE-LEADER WARM-UP AND COOL-DOWN

Suitable for Key Stages 2 and 3 (ages 7 to 14).

Area

Any indoor or outdoor area which allows participants to move about freely at a jogging pace.

Equipment

• Two hoops • Activity cards (front: descriptions of mobility exercises, pulse-raising or -lowering activities or stretches; reverse: blank) • Music machine and music (optional) • Examples of activity cards (see table 6.4; you can make photocopies of table 6.4 for participants as needed)

Warm-Up

1. Participants work in groups of four to six. Number each member of the group.
2. Call out a number from one to six (or one to four). The appropriate participant from each group proceeds to the "mobility or pulse-raising" hoop and selects an activity card. The participant replaces the card in the hoop before returning to the group to lead them through the particular activity prescribed.
3. As soon as you call out another number, the participant chosen leaves the group. While he or she is selecting another activity card, the rest of the group continues with the previous exercise.
4. If a participant selects an activity card that has already been completed by the group, he or she chooses another card.
5. As soon as the group has completed all of the cards in the "mobility or pulse-raising" hoop, the group continues to work in the same way, but this time selects activity cards from the "pulse-raising or stretching" hoop. Participants hold each stretch still for 6 to 10 seconds.

Table 6.4	Examples of Activity Cards for Change-the-Leader Warm-Up and Cool-Down
Mobility and pulse-raising or -lowering activities	**Pulse-raising or -lowering activities and stretches**
Marching	Sidestepping, marching, brisk walking
Hip circles	Stretch muscles in front of upper leg
Arm circles (forwards or backwards)	Stretch muscles in back of upper leg
Side bends	Stretch muscles on inside of upper leg
Upper-body twists	Stretch upper-back muscles
Head tilts and turns	Stretch muscles in back of upper arm
Brisk walking	Stretch muscles across chest
Jogging	Stretch muscles in back of lower leg

Notes

1. Use music to accompany the activity. Participants can change from mobility or pulse-raising activities to pulse-raising or stretches after a track lasting three to four minutes.
2. The amount of direction and guidance on the activity cards depends on the participants' level of knowledge and understanding. Examples of cards for experienced groups are shown in table 6.5 (you can make photocopies of table 6.5 for participants as needed).
3. This warm-up allows you to observe and assess, as well as to give help and advice where appropriate.
4. Ask participants to perform the warm-up activities in pairs or individually in order for detailed assessment of learning to take place. More experienced individuals should be able to make their own decisions about the appropriate length of time to spend on each warm-up exercise before selecting another activity card or moving to the next hoop. Background music might be particularly suitable for this variation.

Cool-Down

You can use the same task, with participants selecting cards from the "pulse-raising or -lowering and stretches" hoop. Instruct participants that for the purpose of the cool-down, the intensity of the activities on the cards should decrease rather than increase. The group should hold each stretch still for 10 to 20 seconds.

| Table 6.5 | Examples of Activity Cards for Change-the-Leader Warm-Up and Cool-Down for More Experienced Participants |

Mobility and pulse-raising or -lowering activities	Pulse-raising or -lowering activities and stretches
A high-impact pulse raiser which travels off the spot.	A low-impact pulse raiser which stays on the spot.
A low-impact pulse raiser which also mobilises impacts.	A pulse raiser that mixes high and low shoulders.
A low-impact pulse raiser which stays on the spot.	Calf stretch combined with triceps stretch.
A pulse raiser that mixes high- and low-impact activities.	Quadriceps stretch. Hamstrings stretch.
Mobility exercises for the spine.	Pectorals stretch combined with adductor stretch.
Mobility exercises for the hips.	Trapezius and rhomboids stretch.

BALL POSSESSION WARM-UP AND COOL-DOWN

Suitable for Key Stages 2 and 3 (ages 7 to 14).

Area

Any indoor or outdoor area which is large enough to allow participants to move freely while jogging. Grid, pitch or court lines are helpful.

Equipment

- One ball per pair (choose equipment which reflects the main activity in the session (e.g., basketball, football, rugby ball)) • Activity cones • Three or four bibs or bands • Whistle

Warm-Up

1. In pairs, participants jog and transport the ball with them in an appropriate manner (e.g., dribbling a basketball or football, or carrying a rugby ball). Ask participants to avoid contacting others by travelling into spaces and passing the ball whenever their partner indicates that they are ready to receive it (e.g., by showing the palms of their hand to their partner).

2. Periodically stop the group and demonstrate a mobility exercise using the ball. Participants perform these activities with their partner before recommencing travelling. Table 6.6 provides examples of mobility activities that you could use.

3. When participants have mobilised the appropriate joints, give each pair two cones or bibs to make a "goal" anywhere in the area. Then ask them to travel around the entire area and to pass the ball to each other between all the goals they have made. The participant who does not have possession of the ball decides which goal they are going to next. The whole process should be continuous. Encourage participants to make quick, accurate passes.

Table 6.6   Ball Possession Warm-Up

Activity	Joints mobilised
10 chest or overhead passes with a partner. Standing back to back, pass the ball between the legs and overhead (keeping legs bent) 10 times.	Shoulders, elbows, wrists Spine, shoulders, elbows, wrists
Standing back to back, twist at the waist to pass the ball: 5 passes one way, 5 passes the other way.	Spine, shoulders, elbows, wrists
Bounce the ball under each leg twice and pass the ball to your partner who does the same. Repeat 5 times.	Knees, hips, elbows, wrists
Pass the ball 5 times around your waist one way then 5 times the other way (at the same time circle the hips). Pass ball to partner who does the same.	Knees, hips, elbows, wrists
Pass the ball around your waist, around your head and between your legs in a continuous sequence. Pass the ball to partner who does the same. Repeat 5 times each.	Hips, shoulders, elbows, wrists

4. Participants make as many passes as possible between the different goals in a short time (e.g., 30 seconds). Encourage participants to pass the ball through as many different goals as possible. They cannot pass through the same goal twice in succession. Challenge participants to determine strategies to beat their own score.

5. Call out the location of a muscle (e.g., the back of the upper arm) or the name of a muscle (e.g., triceps). The participants perform the appropriate stretch in pairs. The pairs should support each other where appropriate. Participants should hold each stretch still for 6 to 10 seconds. Alternate the stretches with partner tasks, using travelling and passing in order to keep the body temperature raised.

Notes

The amount of direction and guidance the participants require will depend on their level of knowledge and understanding.

Cool-Down

Ask participants to repeat any of the travelling and passing activities (perhaps on the way back to the changing rooms). Participants should stretch the relevant muscles outside or in the changing rooms and should perform these in a comfortable, relaxed position where possible. They should hold each stretch still for 10 to 20 seconds.

chapter 7

Key Stages 3 and 4 (Ages 11 to 16)

The following warm-ups and cool-downs are appropriate for use with young people at Key Stages 3 and 4 (ages 11 to 16). Many of the ideas enable participants to work independently, so you can observe, assess, correct and give guidance, encouragement and praise.

GENERAL WARM-UP AND COOL-DOWN

Suitable for Key Stages 3 and 4 (ages 11 to 16).

Area

Any indoor or outdoor area.

Equipment

- Board or card (optional)   • Marker pens (optional)   • Worksheets (optional)

Warm-Up

Participants follow the guidelines in table 7.1; you can write the guidelines on a board, large card or on worksheets; or you can make photocopies of table 7.1 for participants as needed. Participants can work individually or in twos or threes. The warm-up should take about 8 to 10 minutes to complete.

Table 7.1	General Warm-Up Suitable for Key Stages 3 and 4 (Ages 11 to 16)
1	Travel around the area (low-intensity activities).
2	On the spot, mobilise your knees, hips and ankles.
3	Travel around the area. While travelling, mobilise your shoulders, elbows and wrists.
4	On the spot, mobilise your neck, upper back and lower back.
5	Travel around the area, performing high- and low-impact activities (low to moderate intensity).
6	Stretch the muscles in the calf and combine these with stretches for the pectorals and triceps muscles. Hold each stretch still for 6-10 seconds.
7	Continue to gradually raise your pulse with activities performed on the spot.
8	Stretch the quadriceps, hip flexors and hamstrings.
9	Travel around the area performing high-impact activities (low to moderate intensity). Use as much of the area as possible.
10	Stretch the adductors and latissimus dorsi. Hold each stretch still for 6-10 seconds.
11	Shake out your arms and legs.

Figure 7.1   Stretch for the muscles in the chest (pectorals) and the upper calf (gastrocnemius).

Figure 7.2   Stretch for the muscles in the back of the upper arm (triceps) and the lower calf (soleus).

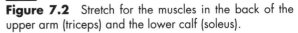

Notes

1. This warm-up is suitable for many activities. You can write it on a large card and place it in a hall or gym for more experienced participants to follow independently at the beginning of lessons, at the start of lunchtime or after school activities.

2. You may have to amend the terminology to suit the needs of the participants.

3. This warm-up assumes that participants are aware of the purpose of mobility, pulse-raising or -lowering and stretching exercises and have learnt how to perform these safely and effectively (e.g., with controlled movements in the mobility and pulse-raising or -lowering exercises and with static stretches).

4. While participants are answering the tasks, you can assess their knowledge and understanding of warming up and cooling down.

Cool-Down

Participants can follow the guidelines in table 7.2 and figures 7.3 and 7.4, which you can write up on a board, large card or on worksheets. Participants can work individually or in twos or threes. The cool-down should take about two to four minutes to complete.

Table 7.2	General Cool-Down Suitable for Key Stages 3 and 4 (Ages 11 to 16)
1	2 moderate-intensity activities (30 seconds each).
2	2 low-intensity activities (30 seconds each).
3	With the support of a partner or a wall, perform stretches for the gastrocnemius, soleus and the quadriceps.
4	Choosing comfortable, relaxed positions, stretch out the • gluteals, • hamstrings, • adductors, • pectorals, and • trapezius and rhomboids. Hold each stretch still for 10-20 seconds.
5	Perform easy mobilising exercises. Wake up the body gently.

Figure 7.3 Stretch for the muscles in the back of the upper leg (hamstrings).

Figure 7.4 Stretch for the muscles inside the upper leg (adductors or groin).

THE ICEBREAKER WARM-UP AND COOL-DOWN

Suitable for Key Stages 3 and 4 (ages 11 to 16).

Area

Any large indoor or outdoor area.

Equipment

- 'Icebreaker' task sheets • Pens or pencils • Large hoops • Beanbags or balls • Skipping ropes • Music machine and music (optional)

Warm-Up

1. Give each participant an Icebreaker worksheet and a pen or pencil. (You can make photocopies of the Icebreaker Warm-Up Worksheet as needed.)
2. Advise them that they can complete the tasks in any order using the equipment provided.
3. Ask the participants to inform you when they have completed the tasks on the sheet (see the Icebreaker Warm-Up Worksheet).
4. After completing the seven tasks, participants stretch out the muscles to be used in the following activity. Participants hold each stretch still for 6 to 10 seconds.

Notes

1. The activity is useful with participants who do not know each other very well. All the activities involve social interaction and require effective communication and co-operation.
2. You may need to modify the tasks depending on the number and previous experience of the participants, the size of the area and the equipment available.
3. Appropriate background music may enhance the atmosphere if the group performs the activity indoors.

Cool-Down

Participants can follow a similar task sheet. Include tasks such as:

1. Ask participants to jog gently or walk quickly with one other person around the area and find out five things about them that you did not know before.
2. Ask participants to walk at a comfortable pace with a different person and tell them the five things that you found out about their previous partner.
3. Participants perform stretches of the muscles predominantly used in the main activity. They hold each stretch still for 10 to 20 seconds and perform the stretches, where possible, in comfortable, relaxed positions.

ICEBREAKER WARM-UP WORKSHEET

Complete the tasks on this sheet in any order.

After finishing each task, the person you work with should sign this sheet.

Task	Signatures
Ask 2 different people (one at a time) to walk briskly on a large pathway of the initial of their first name (use whole area). Walk with them and, if you do not already know their name, try to guess it from the shape of the initial.	Sign here: 1. _____ 2. _____
Ask someone to step or skip through a hoop (taking the hoop over their head and under their feet) 5 times. Copy them exactly with another hoop.	Sign here: _____
Find 4 different people: • someone with blue eyes • someone with brown eyes • someone who is smiling • someone who is wearing similar trainers. Ask each one to throw and catch with you 20 times (i.e., 20 passes).	Sign here: 1. _____ 2. _____ 3. _____ 4. _____
Ask 2 different people (together or one at a time) to follow and copy you. Lead them once around the area using different pathways and arm and leg actions.	Sign here: 1. _____ 2. _____
'Give-me-five' with 3 different people.	Sign here: 1. _____ 2. _____ 3. _____
Jog around the area with someone you have not yet worked with (or do not know very well) and talk to them about their favourite hobby.	Sign here: _____ Favourite hobby: _____
Ask someone to skip with you (either using single ropes or sharing the same rope) for about 1 minute. Try to find something interesting that you have in common.	Sign here: _____ Common interest: _____

SURPRISE SURPRISE WARM-UP AND COOL-DOWN

Suitable for Key Stages 3 and 4 (ages 11 to 16).

Area

Any large indoor or outdoor area.

Equipment

• Blue paper or card (one piece for each participant) • White paper or card (one piece for each participant) • Pens or pencils • Music machine and music (optional) • Variety of equipment (e.g., hoops, skipping ropes, beanbags, balls)

Warm-Up

1. Give each participant one piece of blue paper or card and one piece of white paper or card and a pen or pencil.
2. On the blue piece of paper or card, ask participants to describe or illustrate a mobility exercise and a pulse-raising exercise. On the white piece of paper or card, ask participants to describe or illustrate a pulse-raising exercise and a stretch.
3. Place all the cards in three or four hoops in the centre of the area, face down.
4. Each participant selects a blue card, looks at it and returns it to the hoop.
5. Participants perform the activities described on the blue card for a short time.
6. On completion of this task, the participant selects another card.
7. When participants have completed at least six different blue cards, ask them to select white cards.
8. Each stretch should be held still for 6 to 10 seconds.

Notes

1. This activity involves participants in their own learning (e.g., applying their knowledge and understanding, developing decision-making skills).
2. Guidelines for the participants may include the following:
   • ensure that the pulse-raising activities are active but not too energetic;
   • make use of any equipment provided (e.g., balls, skipping ropes, hoops);
   • keep the tasks simple;
   • think of activities that can be performed alone or with a partner;
   • avoid anything silly or embarrassing.
3. Examples might help participants to design their own idea, for example:
   • Jog around the area and touch all four walls.
   • Perform 20 skips with someone (both jumping in the same rope).
   • Travel three laps of the area using three different ways of travelling on your feet.
4. If the young people do not know each other very well, this activity can help them to interact. For example, ask participants to design activities which involve working with one or two other people.
5. You can develop the activity by introducing a particular theme (e.g., all activities must involve the use of a skipping rope or all activities must involve finding out more about other people in the group).
6. Appropriate background music may enhance the atmosphere if the group performs this warm-up indoors.

Cool-Down

Follow a similar process for the cool-down, in which participants write down suitable pulse-lowering activities and cool-down stretches on cards. Alternatively, you can select cards from the warm-up that are also appropriate for the cool-down. Ask participants to hold cool-down stretches still for 10 to 20 seconds and to perform them, where possible, in comfortable, relaxed positions.

THE PACING WARM-UP AND COOL-DOWN

Suitable for Key Stages 3 and 4 (ages 11 to 16).

Area

An indoor or outdoor area that allows participants to run over a distance of 15 to 30m in a straight line. The area should be large enough for all participants to run at the same time.

Equipment

• Activity cones • Stopwatch • Whistle (optional) • Rate of perceived exertion (RPE) chart (see table 7.3; you can make photocopies of this table as needed)

Warm-Up

1. Place two or more cones about 15 to 30m apart. You can decide the distance or negotiate it with the participants.

2. Ask participants to jog together from one cone to the other and perform this so that it feels very easy (see table 7.3). Jog with the group and, using a stopwatch, time the group's journey and inform them of this time.

3. Participants mobilise their shoulders by performing large, controlled arm circles as they walk back to the starting cone.

4. Challenge the group to repeat the journey between the cones in exactly the same amount of time taken to perform the first journey. Advise participants to pace themselves accurately and discourage them from arriving at the other cone sooner or later than the target time. Assist by calling out the time at the halfway point and at the target time. This will help participants to judge the accuracy of their pacing.

Table 7.3	How the Exercise Feels Chart (Suitable for End of Key Stages 2, 3, and 4, Ages 9 to 16)
Number	**How the exercise feels**
1	Very, very easy
2	Very easy
3	Easy
4	OK
5	Fairly hard
6	Hard
7	Very hard
8	Very, very hard
9	Exhausting
10	Maximum

5. At the end of the second journey, participants mobilise the upper and lower spine by performing upper-body twists and side bends.

6. The participants choose a shorter target time in which the whole group will be able to jog between the cones comfortably. Assist by calling out the time at the halfway point or by calling out the seconds as they pass.

7. At the end of the third journey, the participants mobilise the hips and mime, in a controlled manner, any of the activities in which they will be taking part during the session.

8. Repeat the time challenge two or three more times. On each occasion, encourage the participants to increase the challenge by reducing the target time and to pace themselves accurately without cues.

9. Ask the participants to identify the muscle groups which are used in running and perform their own stretches. They should stretch the muscles in the back of the lower leg (gastrocnemius and soleus), the back of the upper leg (hamstrings), the front of the upper leg (quadriceps) and from the top of the leg to the pelvis or lower back (hip flexors). Ask participants to hold each stretch still for 6 to 10 seconds.

10. Challenge participants to choose their own target time for running fast between the cones. Everyone in the group sets their own challenge and you call out the seconds as the participants are is running. Repeat this two or three times and challenge participants to set faster, slower or the same targets on each journey.

Notes

This is a particularly useful warm-up for track athletics and running sessions. Participants begin to learn about pacing and setting challenges for themselves.

Cool-Down

Participants start by setting themselves personal time targets that will involve them running at a fast pace and working at a high intensity. The participants gradually increase their time targets and aim to be accurate in arriving at the finishing line. The exercise subsequently becomes less intense (e.g., easy or very easy on the RPE scale). Participants can continue to set new targets until they complete the time set in a brisk walking pace. Participants can perform stretches after the pulse has recovered sufficiently from intense exercise but while the muscles are still warm. Participants should stretch the muscles in the back of the lower leg (gastrocnemius and soleus), the back of the upper leg (hamstrings), the front of the upper leg (quadriceps) and from the top of the leg to the pelvis or lower back (hip flexors). They should hold each stretch still for 10 to 20 seconds and perform the stretches, where possible, in comfortable, relaxed positions.

Figure 7.5 Participants jogging around the cones, being timed by the teacher, for the Pacing Warm-Up and Cool-Down drill.

THE BLEEP WARM-UP AND COOL-DOWN

Suitable for Key Stages 3 and 4 (ages 11 to 16).

Area

Any indoor or outdoor area which allows participants to jog in a straight line for at least 20m.

Equipment

- Music machine • Multi-Stage Fitness Test tape (available from the National Coaching Foundation) • Two lines or cones placed 20m apart

Warm-Up

1. Mark out a 20m distance using lines or cones.
2. Explain the use of the Multi-Stage Fitness Test to the participants and allow them to listen to and become familiar with the "bleeps" on the tape.
3. Participants jog 20m shuttles in time with the tape, starting from the beginning of level one and finishing at level three, four or five. The level chosen by participants should enable them to raise their pulse gradually towards the lower end of the cardiovascular training zone (i.e., 55 to 60 percent of maximum heart rate). The participant should consider that the exercise at the end of the warm-up feels OK (on the RPE scale).
4. Participants perform shoulder mobility exercises before or whilst completing the early levels of the tape, and they can perform hip and spine mobility exercises (e.g., controlled knee lifts, hip circles, side bends and upper-body twists) after reaching the selected level.
5. Ask participants to perform appropriate stretches for the muscle groups to be used in the following activity after the shuttle runs. They should hold each stretch still for 6 to 10 seconds. The amount of direction and guidance you give will depend on the level of knowledge and understanding of the participants.

Notes

1. The Multi-Stage Fitness Test is a cardiovascular field test which involves participants running 20m shuttles at a specified pace. The pace is dictated by a bleep on a cassette and gradually increases every minute. At level one, participants have 9 seconds to run 20m.
2. The use of the Multi-Stage Fitness Test in a warm-up context is valuable in that it allows participants to familiarise themselves with the test format before experiencing it under more stressful conditions as a maximal or sub-maximal cardiovascular field test. It also helps participants to learn about and experience pacing. You could design a similar warm-up without the use of the tape, giving participants a certain amount of time to run a specified distance (e.g., 10 seconds to jog the length of the gym). Gradually decrease the time allowed (see the Pacing Warm-Up and Cool-Down on pages 79-80).

Cool-Down

Participants run shuttles or laps of the area in progressively longer time limits (e.g., 6, 8, 10 seconds). Participants stretch the muscle groups used in the main activity. If the main activity is running, participants should stretch the muscles in the back of the lower leg (gastrocnemius and soleus), the back of the upper leg (hamstrings), the front of the upper leg (quadriceps) and from the top of the leg to the pelvis or lower back (hip flexors). They should hold each stretch still for 10 to 20 seconds and perform them, where possible, in comfortable, relaxed positions. The range of stretches and the level of direction you give will depend on the participants' knowledge and understanding.

Suitable for Key Stages 3 and 4 (ages 11 to 16).

Area

Indoor or outdoor space which allows participants room to jog freely amongst each other.

Equipment

- Use tennis, badminton or squash rackets in the stretching section (optional)

Warm-Up

1. Participants jog forwards and backwards along the outline of a large "T" shape on the ground. Participants stop and mobilise the elbows and shoulders by miming a slow and controlled tennis serve or badminton overhead clear. This sequence needs to be performed on both sides of the body. Remind the participants of the teaching points associated with the performance of the tennis serve or badminton overhead clear.

2. Participants jog the outline of the "T" shape again.

3. Participants stop and mobilise the upper back by placing both hands on the shoulders and twisting from the waist to look over alternate shoulders. They should repeat this several times.

4. Participants mobilise the lower back by placing their hands on their hips and gently bending directly to one side and then returning to an upright position before bending to the other side. They should repeat this several times.

5. Participants sidestep along the outline of the "T" shape.

6. Participants stop and find a balanced standing position. They draw a large circle with the hips to the right and to the left.

7. Participants travel anywhere in the space using "Greek-style" travelling (feet alternately stepping in front and behind).

8. Participants perform stretches for the major muscles used in tennis or badminton and alternate these with pulse-raising activities, such as a mixture of sidestepping, jogging in different directions and "Greek-style" travelling. Participants should stretch the muscles on the inside of the upper thigh (groin or adductors), in the back of the lower leg (calf), back of the upper leg (hamstrings), the front of the upper leg (quadriceps), the shoulders (deltoids), the back of the upper arm (triceps), the upper back (trapezius and rhomboids), the sides of the torso (obliques and latissimus dorsi) and the chest (pectorals). Ask participants to hold each stretch still for 6 to 10 seconds. Participants can use the racket to assist appropriate stretches (see figures 7.6, 7.7 and 7.8).

Figure 7.6 Stretch with a racket for the muscles in the back of the upper arm (triceps).

Figure 7.7 Stretch with a racket for the muscles across the chest (pectorals).

Figure 7.8 Stretch with a racket for the muscles across the upper back (trapezius).

9. Follow the stretches by more energetic activities such as:

- Jogging slowly on the spot and at intervals including 10 fast running steps and then slowing down again. Repeat this several times.

- Running towards a set point in a straight line and then sidestepping away from it using the same pathway. When participants return to the starting position, they mime a "smashing" action with their dominant hand and then run forwards again. The whole process is continuous and can be performed at a rapid speed. Participants can also try to perform this sequence with their non-dominant hand.

- Participants perform a mimed backhand or forehand to one side of their body and then shuffle, gallop or run a short distance before repeating the mime of this shot to the other side. This process can be continuous and can be performed rapidly if desired.

Cool-Down

Competent racket players can lower their pulse by playing co-operative rallies (i.e., hitting to their opponent in a controlled manner using less powerful versions of the shots used in the main activity). Less experienced players can lower the pulse by performing any of the appropriate travelling actions described earlier. They can mime the action of the racket where appropriate and gradually decrease the intensity of these actions by reducing the speed, the distance travelled and the size of the movements they use. Participants should stretch the major muscle groups used in the game after the pulse-lowering activities. They should hold each stretch still for 10 to 20 seconds.

PERCEIVED EXERTION WARM-UP AND COOL-DOWN

Suitable for Key Stages 2, 3 and 4 (ages 7 to 16).

Area

This depends on the context in which it is used. This warm-up is particularly relevant preparation for swimming and running events but could also be used for games activities (e.g., dribbling a ball) or for gymnastics and dance (performing set motifs or sequences of movements repeatedly).

Equipment

Rate of perceived exertion (RPE) (or how does the exercise feel?) chart, or sufficient small copies for reference by groups and individuals (see table 7.3).

Warm-Up

1. Show participants an RPE (or how does the exercise feel?) chart and explain how the chart can help them to increase their exercise intensity in a manner that is appropriate for them.

2. Ask participants to start their warm-up by performing activities (e.g., swimming widths or lengths of a pool, dribbling a ball, brisk walking or jogging) at a pace that feels 'very easy'.

3. If participants choose running, they can mobilise their shoulders while exercising at a low intensity. If they choose a sport, replicating the sport action at a low intensity will mobilise the joints to be used.

4. Indicate when participants should gradually increase the intensity of the exercise by referring to the words that appear progressively higher up the RPE chart (e.g., jog one lap of the track so that the exercise feels 'easy', jog another lap of the track so that the exercise feels 'OK' or 'fairly hard'). Individuals should try to be honest about how they feel so the exercise does not become too easy or too strenuous.

5. Participants should perform relevant stretches and hold each stretch still for 6 to 10 seconds.

6. Challenge participants to increase the exercise intensity again (e.g., so that the exercise feels fairly hard or hard). When the muscles have been stretched and the body systems have been prepared for action, it is safe to work at higher intensities.

Notes

1. A perceived rate of exertion chart is composed of a number scale on one side and a word chart on the other, which refer to how hard or easy exercise feels to the individual. Participants can be encouraged to design their own charts using vocabulary that is familiar to them. Table 7.3 provides an example.

2. The amount of direction and guidance you give depends on the level of knowledge and understanding of the participants.

Cool-Down

Participants work initially at an intensity that feels 'hard' and gradually reduce the intensity of the exercise until it feels 'very easy'. Reducing the intensity of the exercise involves making the muscle actions smaller, travelling over a smaller distance, performing the exercise at a slower pace, or any combination of these factors. Participants should hold each of the cool-down stretches still for 10 to 20 seconds in comfortable, relaxed positions where possible.

THE CIRCLE WARM-UP AND COOL-DOWN

Suitable for Key Stages 3 and 4 (ages 11 to 16).

Area

Any indoor or outdoor area which provides sufficient space for the group to form circles of 8 to12 participants.

Equipment

- Cards can be used for this activity but are not essential. Figure 7.9 shows example cards.

Warm-Up

1. Divide participants into groups of 8 to12 and ask them to form a circle in their group.
2. Place the prepared cards in the centre of each group.
3. One participant from each group selects and removes one card from the centre of the circle and begins to perform the mobility or pulse-raising activity it describes. The other members of the group copy him or her.
4. At your signal, the participant leading the exercise calls out the name of someone else in the group, who then selects another card from the centre of the circle. The group members continue to perform the previous exercise until the individual chosen is ready to lead them through the new exercise.
5. This process continues until the group has used all the cards in the centre of the circle.
6. Follow a similar procedure which uses cards indicating the muscle groups to be stretched. You can make these cards appropriate to the knowledge and understanding of the participants (e.g., stretch the back of the upper leg or stretch the hamstrings). Participant should hold each stretch still for 6 to 10 seconds.

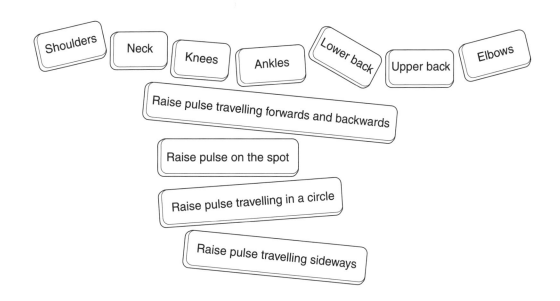

Figure 7.9   Examples of activity cards for the Circle Warm-Up and Cool-Down drill.

Notes

1. For less experienced groups, the directions on the cards can be more specific (e.g., circle shoulders backwards, lift knees high in a marching action, walk four steps forwards and clap, walk four steps backwards and clap).

2. You can call out the instructions instead of writing them onto cards. When you call out a new activity, the participant leading the previous exercise chooses a new leader.

3. Use a die instead of the prepared cards. A central sheet could indicate warm-up exercises to be performed for each number thrown (see table 7.4). The pulse-raising and mobility exercises could be alternated but must be performed before the stretches. Alternate the stretches with more pulse-raising exercises. Because of the random nature of the die throw, you should announce at a certain point in the warm-up that the next leader should perform an exercise for a body part that has not yet been mobilised or stretched. This should ensure that groups cover all the exercises.

4. The group can perform the activities to motivating music.

Cool-Down

Perform the same activity using cards that describe pulse-lowering activities and stretches. The group should perform pulse-lowering activities at moderate to low intensity. They should hold each stretch still for 10 to 20 seconds and perform the stretches, where possible, in comfortable, relaxed positions.

Table 7.4	Activities for the Circle Warm-Up		
Die number	**Mobility**	**Pulse raiser**	**Stretch**
1	Shoulders	Travel forwards	Hamstrings
2	Hips	On the spot	Quadriceps
3	Spine	Sideways	Gastrocnemius
4	Elbows	In a circle	Adductors
5	Ankles	Travel backwards	Pectorals
6	Knees	On the spot	Trapezius

MILE WARM-UP CHALLENGE

Suitable for Key Stages 3 and 4 (ages 11 to 16).

Area

A running track or any large area marked out with cones to calculate 1,500m.

Equipment

- Stopwatches (one per small group or pair) • Cones • Instruction sheets

Warm-Up

1. Give each participant an instruction sheet. Participants start the challenge at an appropriate level for themselves and build up gradually over several weeks to running a mile (see table 7.5). Participants can start anywhere on the track but need to mark their starting position.

2. Participants can work in pairs, small groups or individually. Participants need access to a stopwatch. The cones might be useful as 100m markers for Levels 4 and 5.

Notes

Assist individuals who need help with stretching techniques or with motivation.

Table 7.5	The Mile Warm-Up Challenge
	• The challenge is for you to build gradually to jog a mile without stopping. • It is important that you work at a pace that suits you. • The jogging should feel energetic but should not be uncomfortable or painful. • Choose your own starting level and attempt to move up one level each week. After each level talk to a friend about how the exercise felt. It should get easier each week. If the challenge is not enough, double everything and go for 2 miles!
Level 1	1 lap–brisk walk. 2 laps–alternate–jog for 30 seconds, brisk walk for 30 seconds. 1 lap–brisk walk. Stretch the muscles in the back of the lower leg and in the front of the upper leg. Hold each stretch still for 6-10 seconds.
Level 2	1 lap–brisk walk. 2 laps–alternate–jog for 45 seconds, brisk walk for 15 seconds. 1 lap–brisk walk. Stretch the muscles in the back of the lower leg and in the front of the upper leg. Hold each stretch still for 6-10 seconds.
Level 3	Half a lap–brisk walk. 3 laps–alternate–jog for 45 seconds, brisk walk for 15 seconds. Half a lap–brisk walk. Stretch the muscles in the back of the lower leg and in the front of the upper leg. Hold each stretch still for 6-10 seconds.
Level 4	100m brisk walk, 100m jog, 100m brisk walk. 2 laps of the track jogging all the way. 100m brisk walk, 100m jog, 100m brisk walk, 100m jog. Stretch the muscles in the back of the lower leg and in the front of the upper leg. Hold each stretch still for 6-10 seconds.
Level 5	3 laps jog. Stretch the muscles in the back of the lower leg and in the front of the upper leg. Hold each stretch still for 6-10 seconds.
Level 6	100m very slow jog. 3-and-a-half laps jogging. This is a whole mile–congratulations! Stretch the muscles in the back of the lower leg and in the front of the upper leg. Hold each stretch still for 6-10 seconds.

ZIGZAG WARM-UP AND COOL-DOWN

Suitable for Key Stage 3 (ages 11 to 14).

Area

Large outdoor area or a smaller space indoors is possible.

Equipment

- Five cones of different colours or five numbered cones.
- Red posters naming joints (to attach to the cones; see table 7.6).
- Blue posters naming location of muscles (e.g., back of upper leg; see table 7.6).

Table 7.6	Zigzag Warm-Up and Cool-Down Activities

Red	*Blue*
Hips	Back of the lower leg
Knees	Back of the upper leg
Spine	Inside the upper leg
Shoulders	Across the chest
Elbows	Across the upper back

Warm-Up

1. Set out the cones as shown in figure 7.10. The distance between the cones can be as large as desired, although half the area of an outdoor grass pitch should be sufficient.
2. The participants can work in small groups, pairs or individually.
3. Participants jog between the cones. They cannot go directly to the two cones on either side of the one that they have just visited. They cannot visit the same cone twice during one circuit of the course. Instruct participants to start at different cones at the beginning of the warm-up.
4. When participants arrive at a cone, they mobilise the joint indicated on the card and then continue jogging to their next chosen cone.
5. When they have completed one circuit of the cones, they begin another circuit and this time stretch the muscles as indicated on the cards. They should hold each stretch still for 6 to 10 seconds.

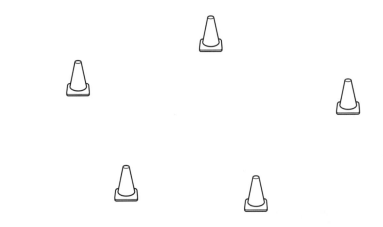

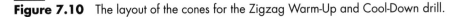

Figure 7.10   The layout of the cones for the Zigzag Warm-Up and Cool-Down drill.

Notes

1. Cards can give more specific guidance for young people with limited knowledge or experience (e.g., diagrams of stretches and descriptions of specific mobility exercises for joints; see figures 7.11 and 7.12).

2. Encourage the participants to vary the travelling actions between the cones (e.g., marching, sidestepping, galloping, crossing feet over).

Cool-Down

Perform the cool-down using the blue muscle location cards. The participants jog or walk briskly between the cones and when they reach a cone they stretch the muscle indicated on the card. They should hold the cool-down stretches still for 10 to 20 seconds.

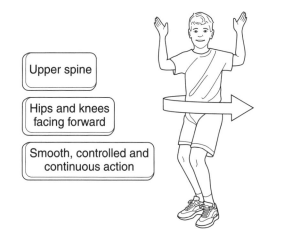

Figure 7.11 Examples of red cards showing the joints and how to mobilise them.

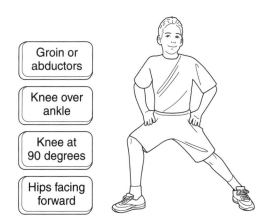

Figure 7.12 Examples of blue cards showing muscle location with diagrams of the corresponding stretch.

Suitable for Key Stages 3 and 4 (ages 11 to 16).

Area

Any indoor or outdoor area.

Equipment

- None

Warm-Up

1. In groups of three, participants number themselves one, two and three.
2. Number one leads the other members of the group through mobility exercises for the main joints (i.e., the ankles, knees, hips, spine, shoulders and elbows).
3. Number two leads appropriate pulse-raising activities. They perform these activities on the spot or travelling.
4. Number three leads stretching exercises for the main muscle groups (e.g., the back of the lower leg (calves), the back of the upper leg (hamstrings), the front of the upper leg (quadriceps), the inside of the upper leg (groin or adductors), the chest (pectorals), back of the upper arm (triceps) and the upper back (trapezius and rhomboids)). They should hold each stretch still for 6 to 10 seconds.

Notes

1. You can assess the participants' knowledge and understanding whilst they are working.
2. The amount of direction and guidance you give will depend on the participants' level of knowledge and understanding.
3. Participants can perform the warm-up to appropriate music. The music for mobility exercises should encourage controlled movement of the joints, the music for pulse-raising or -lowering should be lively and motivating, and the music for stretching should be calm to encourage held stretches.
4. The participants could be given the same task for a specific sport or activity (e.g., design a warm-up for rugby, volleyball, aerobics, circuit training, skipping). You can assess their ability to place the warm-up in a specific context and to select mobility and pulse-raising activities relevant for the sport and appropriate stretches.
5. Ask groups to show their designed warm-ups and cool-downs to other groups who give appropriate feedback based on specified observation criteria written on prepared cards.

   Evaluating a warm-up designed by another group
   - Which joints are mobilised?
   - Are the joints mobilised in a controlled way?
   - Is the pulse raised gradually?
   - Do any of the mobility and pulse-raising activities reflect a particular sport?
   - Which muscle groups are stretched?
   - Are each of the stretches held still for 6 to 10 seconds?

Evaluating a cool-down designed by another group

- Did you keep your major leg muscles working during the pulse-lowering activities?
- Did the cool-down lower your pulse gradually?
- Did you stretch all the main muscle groups used in the activity?
- Did you hold the stretches still in a relaxed position for 10 to 20 seconds?

Cool-Down

1. Ask participants to lead sections of the cool-down (e.g., number one leads the pulse-lowering activities; number two leads the stretches for the lower body; number three leads the stretches for the trunk and upper body).

2. They should hold each stretch still for 10 to 20 seconds and they should perform each in comfortable, relaxed positions.

Suitable for Key Stages 3 and 4 (ages 11 to 16).

Area

Indoor space that allows participants sufficient room to perform the exercises without contacting others.

Equipment

- Music machine and music   • Mats

Warm-Up

1. Participants stand facing you. Lead the participants through a posture check. This involves a clear demonstration and advice concerning the correct technique, while the class members practice. Inform participants of the importance of maintaining a good postural position whilst performing the exercises to follow. The teaching points for the posture check may include:
    - Keep feet a shoulder-width apart.
    - Slightly bend the knees, but do not lock them.
    - Keep the tummy muscles tight and the spine in natural alignment.
    - Keep the shoulders down, back and relaxed.
    - Keep the hips level and facing forwards.

2. Lead the group through a series of exercises to music that mobilise the joints and raise the pulse. The exercises suggested should follow the beat of the music and should be repeated several times before changing to the next set of movements. Use music with a lively, regular beat (about 120 beats per minute). Make transitions between the exercises by
    - changing to the next movement after the group has completed a certain number of the previous exercise;
    - changing to the next exercise according to the phrasing of the music (e.g., changing from the verse to the chorus).

3. The following are suggestions for mobility and pulse-raising exercises:
    - Walk forwards for four counts and backwards for four counts with a clap on "four" each time.
    - Jog anticlockwise in a personal circle for eight counts, performing bicep curl actions with the arms; repeat, travelling clockwise.
    - Perform eight alternate knee lifts touching each knee with the opposite hand.
    - Circle the hips, four counts one way and four counts the other way.
    - Perform four upper-body twists and four side bends (coming back to the upright standing position after each twist and bend).
    - Take four side steps to the left with shoulders circling backwards; repeat to the right.

4. On completion of the mobility and pulse-raising exercises, lead the group through appropriate warm-up stretches. They should hold each stretch still for 6 to 10 seconds. Perform the sequence of stretches to some calmer music and ensure that the transitions between the stretches are smooth in order that the participant can move easily from one position to the next. Suitable sequences for stretches are:

    Sequence one
    - Left hamstring,
    - Right soleus,
    - Right gastrocnemius, and
    - Right quadriceps.

Repeat the stretches mentioned earlier on the other side of the body.

Sequence two

- Groin,
- Right triceps,
- Right latissimus dorsi and obliques,
- Left triceps,
- Left latissimus dorsi and obliques,
- Trapezius and rhomboids, and
- Pectorals.

Notes

Provide teaching points concerning exercise technique (see table 7.7) as well as instructions concerning which exercises to perform.

Table 7.7	Examples of Instructions and Teaching Points for Exercise to Music Warm-Up
Instructions	**Teaching points**
Lift alternate knees.	Keep the back straight and upright.
	Contact the floor softly.
	Bend the supporting knee.
Twist upper body.	Keep the hips and knees facing forwards.
	Keep the movements smooth and controlled.

Cool-Down

Lead the group through a series of pulse-lowering exercises that gradually decrease in intensity. Repeat each set of exercises several times to the beat of the music before changing to the next exercise. The following are examples of a set of exercises that gradually decrease in intensity:

- Four high-impact jumping jacks (astride jumps) followed by eight energetic marches on the spot with high knee lifts and arms pumping.
- Four low-impact astride jumps (i.e., step alternate feet out to the side) with large arm movements (arms taken to head height) followed by eight less energetic marches on the spot with arms and knees lower.
- Four low-impact jumping jacks (i.e., step alternate feet out to the side) with arms up to about shoulder height followed by eight marches on the spot with arms relaxed.

Follow this with a sequence of stretches. Accompany the stretches by calm music and perform them, where possible, in comfortable and relaxed positions on exercise mats. Hold each stretch still for 10 to 20 seconds. Demonstrate the stretches to groups of beginners, but with more experienced groups you might be able to talk the participants through the necessary transitions. A suitable sequence for stretches might be as follows:

- gastrocnemius and soleus (can be performed in a standing position using the support of a wall if desired),
- adductors (seated),
- latissimus dorsi and obliques (seated),
- right triceps (seated),
- trapezius and rhomboids (seated),

- latissimus dorsi and obliques (seated),
- left triceps (seated),
- pectorals (seated),
- gluteus maximus (lying),
- right hamstrings (lying),
- right abductors (lying),
- right gluteus maximus (lying),
- left abductors (lying), and
- right quadriceps (lying).

Allow participants, if appropriate, a few moments to lie in any relaxing position with their eyes closed. Instruct participants to return very slowly to a standing position and lead them through some simple exercises that help them to wake up. These exercises should be easy to follow and of low intensity. The following exercises are suitable for use in this part of the cool-down. They should follow the beat of the motivating music:

- Walk forwards for four counts and backwards for four counts with a clap on "four" each time.
- Step touch (step one foot to the side and bring the other to join it, then repeat to the other side), clicking fingers in a relaxed manner at waist height.
- Lift the heels gently on the spot and shake out the arms.

CIRCUIT TRAINING WARM-UP AND COOL-DOWN

Suitable for Key Stages 3 and 4 (ages 11 to 16).

Area

Any indoor area.

Equipment

- None

Warm-Up

1. Participants march or jog on the spot or travel in the area and, at the same time, perform exercises to mobilise the shoulders (e.g., shoulder circles, shoulder shrugs, arm circles).
2. Participants perform mobility exercises on the spot for the neck, upper back and lower back (e.g., head tilts, side bends and upper-body twists). These exercises should be performed in a smooth and controlled manner.
3. Call out circuit-training or weight-training exercises for the upper body for participants to mime as they jog or march on the spot, for example, biceps curls, upright row, shoulder press, deltoid raises (to the side, in front and behind).
4. Participants perform mobility exercises for the hips (e.g., knee lifts, hip circles).
5. Participants stretch out the muscles to be used in the circuit, for example, the muscles along the length of the spine (erector spinae), in the back of the upper arm (triceps), across the chest (pectorals), in the shoulders (deltoids) and the upper back (trapezius and rhomboids). If the circuit involves cardiovascular work or lower-body work, include stretches for the muscles in the back of the lower leg (calves), the back of the upper leg (hamstrings), the front of the upper leg (quadriceps), the inside of the upper leg (groin or adductors) and the outside of the upper leg (abductors). Ask participants to hold each stretch still for 6 to 10 seconds.
6. Participants run on the spot using their arms vigorously.

Notes

1. Appropriate music can enhance the warm-up.
2. Adapt the warm-up and cool-down for resistance training by asking participants to mime specific resistance-training actions, such as bench presses and dumbbell flyes.

Cool-Down

Participants jog or walk in the area and mime some or all of the upper-body actions used in the circuit-training stations, for example, biceps curls, triceps dips or pushbacks, shoulder presses, deltoid raises (to the side, in front and behind). These should be easy, continuous, rhythmic actions.

Participants stretch each of the major muscle groups used in the circuit, for example, the abdominals (rectus abdominis and obliques), long back muscles (erector spinae), the triceps (back of the upper arm), the chest (pectorals), the shoulders (deltoids) and the upper back (trapezius and rhomboids). If the circuit involved cardiovascular work or lower-body work, include stretches for the calf muscles (back of the lower leg), the hamstrings (back of the upper leg), quadriceps (front of the upper leg), groin (inside of the upper leg or adductors) and abductors (outside of the upper leg). Participants should hold each stretch still for 10 to 20 seconds and perform each in comfortable, relaxed positions, preferably making use of any mats set out for the circuit.

glossary

abduction—movement away from the mid-line of the body (e.g., raising an arm or leg sideways).

abductors—muscles on the outside of the thigh (gluteus medius and gluteus minimus) responsible for lifting the leg sideways (hip abduction).

adduction—movement towards the mid-line of the body.

adductors—muscles on the inside of the thigh responsible for hip adduction, also known as the groin muscles.

aerobic activity—an activity which uses the large muscles of the body continuously for long periods of time, for example, jogging, cycling, swimming, brisk walking, dancing, skipping. During such exercise, oxygen supply is plentiful and energy production takes place in the presence of oxygen.

agonist—the muscle responsible for the joint action (sometimes referred to as the prime mover), for example, the biceps is the agonist muscle, or prime mover, for bending the arm (elbow flexion).

alignment—the natural (anatomically correct) position of the bones and joints.

anaerobic activity—an activity that is intensive and is carried out over a short period of time, for example, 100m sprint. During anaerobic activity, the energy demands exceed the body's ability to supply sufficient oxygen. Energy production takes place predominantly in the absence of oxygen.

antagonist—the muscle group that relaxes to allow the agonist, or prime mover, to contract, for example, the triceps is the antagonist during elbow flexion.

ball and socket joint—a joint, such as the shoulder or hip, which allows movement in all directions (flexion, extension, abduction, adduction, rotation, circumduction).

ballistic stretching—bouncing in stretched positions. Not a recommended method of stretching for most people.

blood pooling—the effect of standing still after energetic exercise in which the increased blood circulation collects in the lower limbs. This can be problematic and can result in a feeling of dizziness and nausea.

cardiovascular system—the heart, blood vessels and circulatory system. Also referred to as the cardiorespiratory system.

carotid pulse—the pulse detected at the carotid artery situated at the side of the neck.

circumduction—movement of a joint that combines flexion, extension, abduction and adduction. Circumduction occurs around the hip and shoulder joints.

cool-down—a process that helps the body to recover from exercise safely and comfortably.

DOMS—an acronym for delayed onset muscular soreness, which refers to post-exercise muscular stiffness and soreness.

duration—the length of time spent exercising.

dynamic flexibility—the ability to use a range of joint movement in the performance of an activity at either a normal or a rapid speed.

erector spinae—the long back muscles that are responsible for spinal extension.

extension—straightening of a joint.

flexibility—the range of movement around joints.

flexion—bending of a joint.

gastrocnemius—the upper of the two calf muscles predominantly responsible for lifting the heel (ankle extension or plantarflexion) and bending the leg (knee flexion).

gluteals—a group of muscles in the backside and outer thigh (gluteus maximus, gluteus medius and gluteus minimus) predominantly responsible for hip extension and hip abduction.

golgi tendon organs—these are sensory receptors responsible for detecting tension on a tendon. When excessive tension is placed on a tendon, an impulse is sent to the muscle causing it to relax. This is known as the inverse myotatic reflex or autogenic inhibition.

groin muscles—the muscles on the inside of the thigh otherwise known as the adductors, which are predominantly responsible for hip adduction.

haemoglobin—a complex protein within red blood corpuscles that readily combines with oxygen and helps to transport oxygen around the body.

hamstrings—a group of muscles in the back of the upper leg primarily responsible for bending the leg (knee flexion).

health-related exercise—physical activity that results in health enhancement.

heart rate—the number of times the heart beats per minute.

heart rate range—this is the range recommended to maintain or develop cardiovascular health or stamina. It is also known as the target zone.

high-impact activity—any activity in which both feet leave the floor and the full body weight is absorbed on landing, for example, jogging, running, jumping, leaping.

hinge joint—a joint, such as the elbow, knee and ankle, which permits movement in one plane, that is, bending (flexion) and straightening (extension) only.

hip flexors—the iliopsoas muscles which run from the top of the leg (femur) to the pelvic girdle and lower back. These muscles are predominantly responsible for bending at the hip joint (hip flexion).

hyperextension—extreme extension of a joint.

hyperflexion—extreme flexion of a joint.

iliopsoas muscle—a hip flexor muscle.

intensity—this refers to the demands of the exercise on the participant, that is, how hard the exercise is.

isometric—a muscle contraction in which there is no visible joint movement or change in muscle length.

isotonic—a muscle contraction in which there is visible joint movement and a change in muscle length.

lactic acid—a by-product of anaerobic energy production, which causes muscle fatigue and soreness.

latissimus dorsi—large muscles on both sides of the back predominantly responsible for shoulder extension and adduction (drawing arms to side of body).

low-impact activity—any activity in which one foot remains in contact with the floor throughout the activity, for example, walking, marching.

lumbar vertebrae—the five bones in the lower region of the spine.

maximum heart rate—the maximum rate at which the heart can function. For children and young people, this is 200 beats per minute.

mobility exercises—controlled movements of the joints through their natural range of movement.

musculoskeletal system—bones, joints, muscles, tendons, ligaments and connective tissue.

myotatic stretch reflex—a reflex mechanism that occurs whenever a muscle is stretched quickly. The reflex action results in the muscle contracting to avoid any potential damage.

National Curriculum—the legal requirements for the 5 to 16 school curriculum, as detailed within the Education Reform Act 1988.

neuromuscular system—the link between the body's nervous and muscular systems (the "brain-body" link).

obliques—muscles that are situated at the sides of the abdominal (stomach) region which are predominantly responsible for rotating the spine.

passive stretching—stretches that are assisted by applying gentle pressure, usually from another body part such as the hands.

pectorals—the main muscles across the front of the chest predominantly responsible for shoulder flexion (horizontal adduction).

PNF stretching—PNF is an acronym for proprioceptive neuromuscular facilitation, which is an advanced form of stretching.

post-exercise soreness—the muscular stiffness and soreness that may be experienced immediately after exercise or during the following day(s).

preparatory stretches—short, gentle static stretches performed in the warm-up to prepare the muscles to be lengthened in the main activity.

pulse-lowering activities—activities which help the body to recover from exercise. These are generally rhythmic movements of the large muscle groups that gradually decrease in intensity.

pulse-raising activities—activities that prepare the cardiovascular system for more intensive work. These are generally rhythmic movements of the large muscle groups that gradually increase in intensity.

pulse rate—the number of times the heart beats over a set period of time (e.g., over 15 seconds or over 1 minute).

quadriceps—the large muscle group at the front of the upper leg predominantly responsible for straightening the leg (knee extension).

radial pulse—the pulse detected at the radial artery in the wrist.

rate of perceived exertion (RPE)—a rating of intensity focusing on how easy or hard exercise feels to an individual.

reciprocal innervation—the action of muscle pairs in which one muscle (the agonist) contracts and the opposing muscle group (the antagonist) relaxes.

rectus abdominis—the straight abdominal muscle predominantly responsible for curling the trunk (spinal flexion).

rhomboids—muscles in the upper back between the shoulder blades predominantly responsible for drawing the shoulder blades together (adduction of the shoulder girdle).

soleus—the deeper of the two calf muscles predominantly responsible for raising the heel (ankle extension or plantarflexion).

stamina—the ability to continue performing aerobic exercise for a reasonable period of time. Also known as heart health, cardiovascular fitness and cardiorespiratory endurance.

static stretching—stretches that are held still. Static stretching is recommended as the safest and most effective way of lengthening muscle groups and improving flexibility.

synovial fluid—lubricating fluid within the inner lining of the joint capsule.

target zone—the recommended exercise intensity for improving cardiovascular functioning or stamina. Research indicates that this is between 55 and 90 percent of maximum heart rate.

thoracic vertebrae—the 12 vertebrae which form the middle section of the spine (to which the ribs attach).

trapezius—a triangular-shaped muscle group in the upper back predominantly responsible for elevation (lifting), upward rotation and adduction of the scapulae (shoulder blades).

triceps—muscles in the back of the upper arm predominantly responsible for straightening the arm (extension of the elbow joint).

vasodilation—an increase in the diameter of the blood vessels.

venous return—the action of blood returning to the heart from the limbs using the contracting action of the major muscles.

warm-up—a process that involves preparing the body gradually and safely for further exercise.

bibliography

Alter, M.J. (1998). *Sport Stretch. 311 Stretches for 41 Sports.* (2nd ed.). Champaign, IL: Human Kinetics.

American College of Sports Medicine. (1995). *Guidelines for Exercise Testing and Prescription.* (5th ed.). Philadelphia, PA: Williams & Wilkins.

Armstrong, N., and Welsman, J. (1997). *Young People and Physical Activity.* Oxford University Press.

British Association of Advisers and Lecturers in Physical Education (BAALPE). (2000). *Safe Practice in Physical Education.* BAALPE.

Donovan G., McNamara, J., and Gianoli, P. (1988). *Exercise Danger.* Western Australia: Wellness Australia Pty Ltd.

Harris, J. (2000). *Health-Related Exercise in the National Curriculum. Key Stages 1 to 4.* Champaign, IL: Human Kinetics.

Harris, J., and Elbourn, J. (1997). *Teaching Health-Related Exercise at Key Stages 1 and 2.* Champaign, IL: Human Kinetics.

Health Education Authority. (1997). *Young People and Physical Activity.* London: Author.

McAtee, R.E. (1993). *Facilitated Stretching.* Champaign, IL: Human Kinetics.

McNaught-Davis, P. (1986). *Developing Flexibility.* Leeds: National Coaching Foundation.

Norris, C.M. (1994). *Flexibility. Principles and Practice.* London: A & C Black.

Pearson, P. (1998). *Safe and Effective Exercise.* Marlborough, Wiltshire: The Crowood Press.

Smith, B. (1994). *Flexibility for Sport.* Marlborough, Wiltshire: The Crowood Press.

Solveborn, S.-A. (1989). *The Book About Stretching.* Tokyo and New York: Japan Publications Inc.

YMCA Fitness Industry Training. (1994). *Getting It Right. The Y's Guide to Safe and Effective Exercise.* (40-minute video). London: Author.

about the authors

Jill Elbourn and Jo Harris

Jo Harris, PhD, is a senior lecturer in physical education at Loughborough University in Leicestershire, where she has played a major role in the training of physical educators since 1990. Before this, she was involved in teacher education in Cheltenham and taught physical education and health education at the secondary school level for 12 years. She was co-director of the Loughborough Summer School course titled 'Health-Related Exercise in the National Curriculum'. She holds a master's degree in physical education from Birmingham University and a PhD in pedagogy, exercise and children's health from Loughborough University. Jo wrote *Health-Related Exercise in the National Curriculum* and co-authored with Jill Elbourn the highly successful *Teaching Health-Related Exercise at Key Stages 1 and 2*.

Jill Elbourn, MSc, is a freelance educational exercise consultant. She co-authored *Teaching Health-Related Exercise at Key Stages 1 and 2* with Jo Harris and has written several other publications and resources including *Action for Heart Health*, *Fit for TOPs* (for the Youth Sport Trust TOPs programme) and *Planning a Personal Exercise Programme* (YMCA Fitness Industry Training's HRE resource for Key Stage 4 – ages 14 to 16). Jill taught physical education in schools for 12 years and currently designs and leads in-service training courses on health-related exercise and safe exercise practice for school teachers and coaches all over the British Isles. She was awarded a fellowship of the Physical Education Association of the United Kingdom in 1998.